CHATS ON . .
WEDGWOOD WARE

CHATS ON WEDGWOOD WARE : *By* HARRY BARNARD

7294

WITH A COLOURED FRONTISPIECE
AND ILLUSTRATIONS

738
B25

NEW YORK
FREDERICK A. STOKES COMPANY
PUBLISHERS

PRINTED IN GREAT BRITAIN

PORTRAIT OF JOSIAH WEDGWOOD, F.R.S.

(*From the painting by Sir Joshua Reynolds.*)

To follow title-page.

DEDICATED TO THE MEMORY OF

MAJOR CECIL WEDGWOOD, D.S.O

A JUST MASTER AND A TRUE FRIEND ; WHO
EMULATED THE ACTIONS AND IDEALS OF HIS
ILLUSTRIOUS ANCESTOR FOR THE BENEFIT OF
THE POTTERY INDUSTRY AND THE CRAFTSMEN
OF STAFFORDSHIRE ; WHO MADE AT LA
BAISSÉE, ON THE 3RD JULY 1916, THE GREAT
SACRIFICE FOR KING AND COUNTRY DURING
THE GREAT WAR

FOREWORD

IT is necessary that an author should give a reason why his book is put before the reader, and yet the preface is often passed over to get at the more palatable matter beyond. Bear with me, for these covers contain that which is reliable and, I venture to say, quite new to the connoisseurs and collectors of Wedgwood.

When entering upon the writing of another volume to add to the already interesting and useful series of " Chats," a peculiar pleasure gave impetus to the task, for the existing accumulation of books and articles which have appeared upon this subject have almost without exception emanated from " without."

It was a happy idea of the Publishers to approach the actual source, and so secure a volume in which the details and information came from " within."

The mass of literature which has from time to time been published, especially during the past half-century, has come from those who have given much careful study and patient research to the subject, but it is a fact that although they have received and acknowledged assistance from various sources, it has mainly been from collectors and dealers. This is the first account that has been born from " within," that is, from Etruria, the works that Josiah Wedgwood, F.R.S., built in 1769 to carry on and enlarge upon the discoveries and inventions which had their foundation in his Burslem factories during the previous ten years.

The works at Etruria have been under the management of the " Family " ever since, never being without the guiding influence of a Wedgwood through five generations to the present sixth of direct descent.

The traditions are preserved, and in a number of instances the same lineal descent exists among the workpeople, so that it is quite a correct conclusion when we say that the potter's craft in all its branches is as hereditary as any other characteristic.

In the workshops one finds the same love of producing the best, and the same loyalty that existed during the latter part of the eighteenth century.

In the museum upon the works there is a mass of manuscripts, documents, letters, ledgers, workmen's time books, oven count books, registers, books containing mixings, notes and descriptions of processes, and hundreds of other details referring to shapes, tools, and machinery, which all stand as witness to remarks made in this book, although some may come as a revelation, even a shock perhaps, to lovers and collectors of Wedgwood Ware.

The author has had the honour and privilege of connection with the firm of Messrs. Josiah Wedgwood & Sons, Ltd., and the old works at Etruria for over a quarter of a century.

My grateful acknowledgments for helpful interest in a great variety of ways are made to those who have so kindly tendered it.

To Her Majesty the Queen for permission to utilize specimens in her private collection for illustrations, viz. the unique vase produced in colours as a frontispiece, and the black and white reproductions of medallions shown facing pp. 171, 178, 179.

To the Trustees of the British Museum for facilities given to include illustrations of specimens from the Ceramic Section, and to R. L. Hobson, Esq., for kindly assistance.

To the Authorities of the Victoria and Albert Museum for permission to photograph specimens in the department of the Ceramics, and to Bernard Rackham, Esq., for his assistance.

To the Corporation of Stoke-on-Trent for permission to photograph and use specimens from the Hulme Bequest at Burslem.

To Messrs. Josiah Wedgwood & Sons, Ltd., for placing at my service any material that I wished to use in making this book.

To Mr. John Cook, the Curator of the Museum at Etruria, for his willing and valuable help.

To friends who have generously assisted : Messrs. George Miles, Arthur Hayden, Thomas Hartley, and others who have helped to make the publication of this volume possible.

HARRY BARNARD.

HARTSHILL, STOKE-ON-TRENT,
    June 1924.

CONTENTS

CHAPTER I

The allurement of Wedgwood Ware—Popular idea of
Wedgwood Ware—Caution necessary in collecting—
Wedgwood a pioneer—Other wares marked "Wedgwood"
—The wares of contemporary potters—Difficulties of judging "Old Wedgwood"—The best test for judging—The
variations of materials—Difficulty of imitating Wedgwood—Influence of foreign pottery upon Staffordshire's
productions—The Stuart period—The slow progress of
the seventeenth century—The birth of Josiah Wedgwood
—His education—Royal Patronage—The old works—
Etruria Museum.

CHAPTER II

The boy Josiah leaves school—He starts work as a potter—
Learns the craft of "throwing" on the potter's wheel—
His apprenticeship—His rapid progress—His decision to
leave the home works—Partnership with Harrison &
Alders—Improvements effected—A new partnership
with Whieldon—Important workmen—Old Experiment
Book—Salt glazed ware—Early trials—Meaning of
letters impressed on some ware—"Cauliflower" and
"Pineapple" ware—Green glaze—The original mixing
receipt—Old moulds and block patterns—Wedgwood's
persistent self-culture—Patronage and appreciation of

15

CHAPTER V

The refinement and unique quality of the Jasper " body "
—The history of its birth and development—The white
and coloured clays—The " first seedlings "—The difficulties—How Wedgwood looked upon this new departure
—The expenditure of time and money upon perfecting
it—Vases not made during the Wedgwood & Bentley
partnership—First essays in vase making—Tablets for
chimney pieces—Attention to trial cabinet and experiment books—Whimsical Jasper composition—The boast
of a neighbour potter—Continued difficulties—The persistent application necessary to overcome them—The
slow but sure climb to success—Jasper vase making
achieved—The old shape book—The stamp "Wedgwood"
a guarantee—The second Josiah—The progress due to him
—The first shapes—The Portland vase—The Homeric
vase—Wedgwood's estimate of it—His standard of
judgment—The Queen's vase—Wares imitated.

CHAPTER VI

The artistic quality of basaltes—" Fakes "—Busts and
figures in other colours—Half busts and half figures—
Their uses—Other figures stamped 'Wedgwood," but not
Josiah's—The Wedgwoods contemporary with Josiah—
No trace of busts or figures before the days at Etruria—
The start in bust making—The first subjects—Hackwood's
valuable work—Orders from Dublin—Variations and
special " things "—Busts of the later period—The old
pricing list for busts—Unique bust of the Rev. Laurence
Sterne—Wedgwood's desire to make vases rather than
figures—Figures for candlesticks, lamps, etc.—Animal
figures.

CHAPTER VII

The period covered by this class—The zeal and originality
given to its production—The variety of subjects chosen—
Wedgwood's opinion of tablet making—The personal
element—The advantage of Jasper over marble—Its
value and price—Tablets in red and black—Success
dated—An original list of subjects—Flaxman's model—

Appreciation of efforts—White Jasper tablets—The cameo series—Royal patronage and portrait medallions—The adaptation of cameos to seals—Their introduction into various articles of use and ornament—The earlier cameos with enamel grounds—Intaglios—Different ways of mounting the same—Historical cabinets—The Sydney Cove cameo—Extracts from Governor Phillips' letters—The slave cameo—Memorial cameos for Germany—Introduction of cameos into jewellery—Portrait medallions—Illustrious moderns—The classical sets—Flaxman's contribution to the series—Hackwood's share—Admiral Keppel—Dr. Priestley—Sir Isaac Newton—Sir Wm. Hamilton.

CHAPTER VIII

The models that came to Etruria—The resources within—John Flaxman—Father and son—Their connection with Wedgwood—John Flaxman, Junr., R.A.—His work for Wedgwood—Letters referring to it—The muses—The dancing hours—Hackwood's remodelled version—Hackwood's position with regard to all work sent from outside—Flaxman in Rome—His work there—List of Flaxman's models—Hackwood's engagement—His capable work in busts, portraits, cameos and seals—Appreciation of his work—List of his models—The Sydney Cove cameo—Webber—The Portland vase figures—Webber's responsible position—Tebo—Wedgwood's estimate of him—His short stay at Etruria—The harm he did—The craftsmen of Etruria—Boot—Denby—Models supplied but not direct from the artist—Tassie—Joachim Smith—The reason for the sudden stoppage of his work—Voyez—Bacon—Lochee—Pesez—Coward—His pearwood carved models—The models sent from Rome—Devære—His position at Rome—The other Italian artists who made models from the antique—Lady Templetown—Lady Diana Beauclerk — The Gossets — Dassier — Pingo — George Stubbs, R.A.—The modelling he did for Etruria—Models supplied from the plaster model dealers.

CHAPTER IX

The various coloured " bodies " made at Etruria—Pearl " body "—The Red " body "—Cane coloured " body "—

ILLUSTRATIONS

CHAPTER III

CHAPTER VII

BIBLIOGRAPHY

MANY books dealing entirely or partially with Wedgwood and his works have been published, and all are useful books of reference, but even these authoritative works, as will be seen by the revelations in the present volume, contain assertions which cannot now be accepted as correct. Wedgwood bibliographies must be recast.

Recent research among manuscripts which were not available when the books were published has altered the opinion which was then formed. One instance may be quoted : Miss Meteyard, in her reprint of Wedgwood's catalogue of 1787, attaches the names of the artists who produced many of the subjects used as tablets, etc. These do not appear in the original catalogue, and cannot be verified, except in the few instances noted in this book.

GLOSSARY

Basaltes.—The name given to the black porcelain ware by Wedgwood. It is used to describe the ware, a single piece or a collection of pieces, and is also applied to the clay or " body " before firing.

Bats.—Discs of soft clay beaten out flat like pancakes, and used for plate making or placing inside a mould when making a jug, vegetable dish, or other piece of " hollow " ware.

Bisque or Biscuit.—Ware which has been fired once and is terra-cotta. It is the preliminary stage of all earthenware and china.

Blocks.—See Moulds.

Body.—The clay or material in which a piece of ware is made. It is always used in this sense and never as applied to a portion of a vase or other article.

Cameos.—Always used to refer to those in Jasper or other " bodies " made by Wedgwood.

China.—A hard white porcelain " body," in the composition of which there is a large percentage of bone ash, which distinguishes it from porcelain. It is translucent.

Coverdish.—A vegetable dish or other piece of similar shape having a cover.

Covered Pieces.—Any piece of ware having a cover, such as tureen, vegetable dish, jug, teapot, sugar box, etc.

Cream Colour.—The name given to a pale ivory-coloured earthenware.

Earthenware.—Any ware that is opaque, and fired once for " bisque " and a second time for glaze. It may be decorated in three ways : by emboss-ment or relief upon the clay before firing, by painting upon the bisque, or by painting upon the top of the glaze, after the second fire, such decoration being fired again in an enamel kiln.

Enamel.—The vitreous colours that have been fired upon the ware in the kiln.

Engine Turning.—A process of decoration produced mechanically in the turner's lathe by using a species of eccentric chuck. This is done upon the soft clay.

Fettle, Fettling.—The finishing of a piece of ware in the clay state.

Firing, Fire, Fired.—The process of turning clay into pottery by burning it in a special oven or kiln. The heat varies according to the ware, from 800° to 1,250° and the time of firing from 16 hours to 60 hours or more.

Flint.—The natural stone, which is calcined, then crushed and ground to a fine powder. This is used for mixing with the various " bodies," to lessen contraction, whiten, etc.

Fluting.—One of the decorations applied by the engine turning lathe.

Glost, Gloss.—The oven in which the glaze is fired upon the biscuit piece.

Glaze.—A compound of materials applied to a piece of ware, which when fired in the *glost* oven become a thin coating of glass or glaze upon the surface.

Intaglio.—The opposite to a cameo. Made by Wedgwood in various coloured bodies for sealing purposes.

Jasper.—A hard porcelain " body." The name given by Wedgwood to a series of " bodies " in different colours used for his vases, placques, medallions and cameos, generally a coloured ground having a subject or decoration in white relief upon it.

Kiln.—A box or muffle in which ware is put to fire at a low temperature enamel colours or gold. The heat is generally only a bright red in colour, and the actual fire does not come in contact with the ware.

Lug.—An ear or solid piece put on to a piece of ware to lift it by. It is not a handle which has a place through which the fingers or hand can be put.

Marks, Marked.—Always used to denote the stampings to be found on the clay, or the painted signatures or initials on or under the glaze.

Model, Modelling.—The pattern made by the artist in clay. The process of making the pattern. Not to be confused with " moulding " or " throwing."

Moulded, Moulding.—Ware that has been made in a mould. The process of making ware in a mould, and never used to describe either " modelling " or " throwing."

Moulds.—These are made in plaster or clay fired into hard bisque, and are used for pressing or making ware or ornaments. There are three kinds of moulds, the *raised block mould*, which is the pattern from which the "*working*" or hollow mould is made, which is used by the potter for making his ware ; the *hollow block mould*, kept for reproducing purposes ; the *working mould*, made in quantities as required for the potter's use. *Block moulds* are kept to enable standard and reproduction to be maintained.

Oven.—The place where " bisque " or glaze is fired. In Staffordshire the ware, while in the oven, is always enclosed in a " saggar."

Placing.—The process of putting the ware in the " saggar " or in the oven.

Porcelain.—A hard vitreous " body." Any ware which is fired so that its material is non-porous is a porcelain.

Pot Bank, Pot Works.—In Staffordshire, the factory.

Queensware.—The name given to Wedgwood's cream-coloured ware after it had received the Royal Patronage of Queen Charlotte (wife of George III), and has since become a general term for this class of goods.

Saggar.—A corruption of the words " safe guard." A fire-clay box to contain the ware when " placed " in the oven, to protect it from dirt and direct action of the fire or smoke during the process of firing.

Salt Glaze.—Salt glazed ware is produced in one fire, the clay piece being put into the oven or kiln unprotected by any " saggar." When the correct heat is reached (a white heat), salt is thrown into the oven and upon the fires ; this volatilises, and the soda combining with the silica in the clay causes a thin deposit of glass or glaze upon the surface of the piece of ware.

Seconds.—Ware not perfect, but usable, having some slight defect.

Slip or Slop.—Clay and water of the consistency of thick cream, in which state it can be poured into a porous mould, or a piece of clay ware can be dipped into it, and so receive a coating on the surface. In this way the Jasper coloured grounds are often produced. Glaze or enamel for coating surfaces when of the same consistency are often termed " slips."

Stoneware.—Generally a term used to denote salt glaze, although sometimes it is used in connection with any hard vitreous " body."

Throwing.—The process of making ware upon the wheel. It probably gets its name from the action of throwing the ball of soft clay down upon the revolving wheel or flat horizontal disc ; the ball is then trued or centred upon the wheel and worked up with the hands, the potter dexterously pulling up the soft clay and forming the shape he desires entirely in this way. The term " thrown " is applied to ware made in this way, without the aid of any mould.

Turning.—Clay ware, after it has been " thrown " upon the wheel, is allowed to partially harden, and then is passed to the turner, who puts it upon the lathe and shaves it to the desired line, putting in any beads or fillets and burnishing the whole with a hard tool to give it the finished surface.

I

PRELIMINARY
REMARKS

CHATS ON WEDGWOOD WARE

CHAPTER I

PRELIMINARY REMARKS

The allurement of Wedgwood Ware—Popular idea of Wedgwood Ware—Caution necessary in collecting—Wedgwood
a pioneer—Other wares marked "Wedgwood"—The
wares of contemporary potters—Difficulties of judging
Old Wedgwood—The best test for judging—The variations of materials—Difficulty of imitating Wedgwood—
Influence of foreign pottery upon Staffordshire's productions—The Stuart Period—The slow progress of the
seventeenth century—The birth of Josiah Wedgwood—
His education—Royal Patronage—The old works—
Etruria Museum.

WHAT is the allurement of Wedgwood Ware? Why
should so many desire to collect it or possess even a
specimen of it? It has not the advantage of hoary
antiquity such as the Egyptian or even Cypriote
pottery, to examine which seems almost like peering
into the grave; in fact, it is from the tombs that we
derive our knowledge of those treasures. No! the
antiquity of Wedgwood is in comparison quite modern,
and yet it has a mystery which is as alluring, claiming
the attention of the connoisseur. It has always been
preserved in the houses of the comparatively few who
appreciate and recognise excellence of technique, refinement of taste, and delicacy of texture and colour.

Of late years that small circle has become larger, and we find an ever-widening area over which to spread the limited supply. For this reason it is considered that this volume may prove of more than ordinary interest, as it is intended to guide along safe and reliable channels those who have the desire to collect.

The answers to the questions above are to be found when examining a piece of Wedgwood Ware of the best period, say 1780–1790. The quality of the body amazes both the potter and the chemist, the design and decoration delight the artist, the form fascinates.

The career of the man who created such a masterpiece must be worthy of study, surely a genius who could command material and labour to the use and delight of his fellow-men is a Prince of Commerce, and more than a mere maker of money.

True service to an industry brings success, and success is reward. Such is Wedgwood Ware, a delight at the time of its birth, and perhaps at the present it has even a more powerful attraction, as it has held its head high all through the century of progress in ceramics which has followed.

Although many books and magazine articles have been published upon this subject, it still remains true that upon the mention of the word " Wedgwood " the average person at once visualises a blue ware with white figures in relief upon it, and so far has this idea become ingrained in the mind, that the ordinary lover of things ceramic goes farther still and assigns to Wedgwood any vase or pot that is blue and white, whether it be in relief or not, regardless of the technique, shape or design. This practice is still so persistent that it is thought the present volume can in no way overload the correct information already published, and will, it is hoped, add much to the subject for the use of the collector.

The collecting of Wedgwood pottery has increased a hundredfold during the last twenty years, and for that one reason alone it behoves the newly starting collector to be alert and as well informed as possible, for a great mass of Wedgwood, genuine enough from the fact that it has issued from the factory at Etruria, has come into the antique market, much of it very beautiful in colour and workmanship, but of a later period than that which is rightly understood as " Old Wedgwood," namely, pieces made during the lifetime of the Founder of Etruria, Josiah Wedgwood, F.R.S., 1730–1795.

There are many milestones and fingerposts which indicate with certainty the right road to travel, and it is by this way that we intend to go, rigidly refusing to make any deviation into the path of romance. For the reader's guidance we shall state only such facts as can be proved without doubt, thereby silencing any controversy over what may have already appeared in print to the contrary upon any particular point.

In " chatting " upon Wedgwood Ware the whole field of Etruria's efforts must be included, and to do that it will be necessary to come down much farther into the nineteenth century than is generally done by those who have given the subject serious study, for the tendency has been to place as far back as possible any specimen that has been found and added to a collection. In this way many errors have been started and circulated in all good faith.

Josiah Wedgwood, the great English master potter, was a true pioneer ; he was a discoverer ; he made good as he went along, leaving a clear road for others to follow ; his aim was always to leave things better than he found them and to make better pots than had been made before ; to raise the standard of living, of education ; to place the district in which he lived and worked, in communication with the rest of the world, so that the improved product could bring wealth and prosperity to the community. All this is a history by itself and must be left out here, but for our purpose now it will be necessary, without detracting one iota from the just estimate of his wonderful life's work in all its varied activities, to give to his son Josiah, who took the master's position on the works (even before the death of his father), his right place in the sequence of Etruria's productions. Many of the wares, shapes, and designs so prized in collections to-day belong to his period and not to that of the first Josiah. During his régime the Napoleonic Wars affected the whole feeling and trade of this country, and after the Battle of Waterloo the sudden rush of orders and inquiries for English goods led to a vast increase in the manufacture of pottery, among which was some of the finest of Wedgwood Table Earthenware ever " potted." A great deal of this has deservedly found a place in collections to-day.

There are in existence to-day pieces of ware belonging to the eighteenth century which have the name " Wedgwood " impressed upon them, and this has always been the cause of much misunderstanding, even in the highest and most expert circles of collectors. In many cases it is not known, and in most it is not realised, how many manufacturers (in nearly every instance in quite a small way of business) of the name of Wedgwood existed before and contemporary with Josiah Wedgwood ; some of these used the mark WEDGWOOD for their ware. Our public museums have such specimens wrongly ascribed to Josiah, and one feels that this is a fitting opportunity definitely to make this statement, as doubts and uncertainties have been allowed too long to go unnoticed. It is difficult to say how many Wedgwoods were making pottery during the lifetime of the great master potter, Josiah Wedgwood, but it is certain there were seven [1] manufacturers of that name, and it is quite probable twice that number existed. The goods they produced were just the regular and ordinary wares of the period, with here and there some specialities of a more elaborate kind, characterised by a finer texture in the fabric itself with better technique and finish. This may be said more especially with regard to single figures and groups decorated with coloured glazes, and finished with brushwork diaper or marbled painting both under and over the glaze.

Cauliflower, Pineapple [2] and Cabbage Ware, as well as Mottled, Marbled and Agate, were the knowledge and property of all, although they are generally now classed under the one name " Whieldon," but in these products of course Wedgwood had a very definite place. Specimens of his can be recognised with some certainty by those who have studied the subject and are acquainted with his methods of working, details of

[1] See Chapter VI, p. 151.   [2] See illus. facing p. 66.

shape, modelling of handles and spouts, and excellence of potting.

The early pieces of Wedgwood, those made at Burslem between 1759 and 1769, were not marked. This is undoubtedly so in the case of the ornamental Queensware Vases of that period, but as this class of ware was unique and is possessed of distinctive qualities, it is easily identified and not likely to be confused with pieces of later date or those from other factories.

Black Basaltes, or Egyptian Black, as it was at first called, presents great difficulties to the collector, for the popular idea is that a piece of black ware must be Wedgwood as surely as a piece of blue and white jasper is. When it was discovered that there was a demand for black ware, every manufacturer who could at once began to produce it in quantities with varying degrees of success, because of its beauty of texture, its ability to display and accentuate form, its adaptability to contrast or harmonise with any colour scheme, and its overwhelming advantage as a foil to any kind of floral decorations. Some produced original designs and shapes ; many copied or followed (as nearly as they were able) the patterns which had been made by the acknowledged leader, Wedgwood ; and others, again, contented themselves with copying those who had copied others ; till at the end of the list we have that which is not worthy to live at all as specimens of the potter's art.

Here again it is not easy to compute the number of factories making this black ware during Wedgwood's lifetime, but we should not be far wrong if the estimate was given at about twenty. It is safe to say that of

the Black Basaltes ware which left Etruria, much did
so without the mark upon it, and after the practice of
marking was started it was the custom to stamp only
the bottom piece when a vase was composed of three
or four pieces. Even should that section be missing
or broken, the remainder has that about it in detail,
shape, finish and texture which will leave no doubt
in the connoisseur's mind.

For beginners it would be wise to reject any piece,
especially a one-piece article, such as a dish, jug or
bowl, that is not marked.

Red Ware (Rosso Antico) was contemporary with
Basaltes and was made in the same shapes and articles
as far as useful ware is concerned—teapots, flowerpots,
jugs, bowls, etc.

Cane Ware—a vitreous, bisque body, generally
glazed in the interior of all useful pieces, of a deep
buff colour of very fine smooth texture and capable of
taking the most delicate finish at the turner's lathe—
belongs to the first period, that is, Josiah Wedgwood's
lifetime ; but as the production has continued without
break until the present day, great discrimination and
knowledge have to be brought to the selection of pieces
that belong to the earliest period.

Lavender Ware—a glazed earthenware of a full
tinted pale blue colour—was not introduced until about
1850. It was made in all the old shapes of plain and
ornamental table ware, and has the same finish as
much of the " Cane " Ware, although the sharpness
of detail is seen through the transparent glaze.

Drab Ware—a glazed earthenware, varying in colour
according to the heat reached in firing, from a greenish

olive to a fawny brown—was made first in the early part of the nineteenth century, in a range of articles mainly for table use, and with " Cane " shared popularity during the second period, namely, that which is embraced between the dates of the deaths of the first Josiah and the second Josiah, 1795 and 1843 respectively.

Flemish Ware is of a later date still. It is a fine earthenware, glazed and finished as " Drab " and " Lavender," and made in a series of shapes similar in every way. The colour is a grey green, or bluish sage, and varies considerably in the same way as " Cane," " Drab " and " Lavender."

One of the chief difficulties to contend with in judging " Old Wedgwood " is that the would-be purchaser has sometimes little technical knowledge. So many pieces have been skilfully repaired, and in the case of vases portions have been added. It is an almost universal rule that such ornamental objects, especially in jasper, are made up of three or four separate pieces, viz. the body, the cover, the foot and the plinth ; and also it was the practice, as already mentioned, to mark the plinth, the bottom piece, and none of the others. Although the centre piece was perhaps the most important part, its mark would have been hidden when all the parts were assembled and fixed together.

So it occurs repeatedly that a plinth which may be perfectly genuine in age and make is attached to one, two, or three super pieces of fine technique that are of later, even quite modern, date, either of Wedgwood Ware, or some similar manufacture. One very often

finds attached to a plinth, a piece of genuine antique
contemporary with it, but of Adams, Neale, Turner,
Palmer or others, for it must be remembered that
many factories emulated Wedgwood in his endeavour
to produce fine Jasper, some with great success.
Still, to the initiated there is a marked difference,
and " Wedgwood " stands by itself, detracting nothing
from other good work, and is as it were " marked all
over " to those who have the eyes to see, for it has
form, finish, colour and texture which belong alone to
it, and minutiæ of detail occur in one piece which are
reproduced in another, telling plainly the individuality
of the artist.

In a similar way with a cover-dish or vegetable-dish—
the bottom part would have the impressed mark, and
the cover which had received the full design and
decoration be destitute of any mark whatsoever. It
was very usual in the case of the old hand-painted
dinner sets that the dish part of the cover-dish, certainly when it had no lugs or handles, was only decorated by a line or a band and line round.

How many are there outside a " potbank " who could
when handling—say a dozen—ordinary hand-made
pieces, such as vases or tureens, all of the same shape,
design, and size, say, " This, and this, are made by one
man " and " That, and that, by another " ? Yet,
although there is no appreciable difference to either
the seller or the buyer, the workman and the ware-
houseman often can tell, without referring to any
marks, whose work it is.

Such points as these make it so difficult to guide the
collector to a right choice, for it is too obvious at times

that some have not been able to learn anything from former mistakes.

Experience, after all, is the only factor that really counts, and those accustomed to handling all kinds of pottery can usually recognise " Wedgwood " at a glance, aided by touch, for there is much in the feel of a piece, quite apart from texture (which may only denote age—the patina caused by handling and dusting for a hundred years or so)—the weight, the balance and the flow of line as the finger passes over the shape, the variation of colour, the " ring " of the material as it is sounded by the slightest tap, are all points which cannot be transmitted by the most elaborate written instruction.

When a genuine piece of Old Wedgwood Ware is placed in the hand the first sensation is a feeling of surprise, even to those who are in the habit of handling pottery ; and the verdict can at once be given, " It is Wedgwood."

What is the nature of this " surprise " ? An exclamation, " Oh ! how light ! " The material, the thinness, and the balance of the ware, no matter whether it be black or white, all combine to give the feeling of perfect workmanship.

Dealers especially like to have some hard-and-fast rules by which they can identify the ware which comes into their hands, and of course foremost among such aids are marks ; but in dealing with the productions of an old factory where the same marks have been used since the first Wedgwood's time, and still are used, it is quite easy to understand how the slightly informed and inexperienced can be misled. The materials out of which the clays or bodies are made are not stable units; two spadefuls taken from beside each other in the same mine differ; how much more so the same material from two different mines? And again, the strata from which the raw material came one day must be very different when even one or two years' supply has been removed, hence the potter's continual necessity to prove and make trials of every consignment of that which comes into his hands for the purpose of making up his clays.

If this were not so, how easy comparatively would be the manufacturer's task, and why should Wedgwood himself have made thousands of trials to perfect one particular " body," for having once arrived at a standard it is perhaps natural to suppose that a certain amount of latitude was permissible? But this is not so; constant vigilance and continual testing of every batch of material used was necessary even to maintain a certain standard, and his anxiety was always to progress beyond what he had already achieved.

For this reason pieces of ware of the same period may and do vary considerably, and unique specimens occur all along the line; because one specimen may with certain knowledge be put down to a definite date, it is not correct to suppose that another piece belonging to the same period must necessarily present the same features and details.

Workmanship and technique are the best tests after all. Avoid articles which show any signs of bad making or rough workmanship of any kind, shapes which are not true in line, and ornaments which show badly defined detail.

Let it be definitely said that " Old Wedgwood " always shows attention to the minutest detail, whether it be in the more commercial table ware, or the finest of vases, placques and cameos. Of course, the standard was raised as knowledge and experience progressed.

One reason may be advanced why the collection of Wedgwood Ware has an additional advantage over many, if not all, other objects which are selected. We continually hear of imitations, " fakes " and " duds " in furniture, metal work, pictures and fabrics, but a very short apprenticeship will convince that " Wedgwood " cannot be " faked."

There never was a period in the recorded history of England when pottery was not made, and the potters, insignificant though they may have been, have left traces behind in the form of pots, which show clearly that a genuine striving after excellence of some sort or another was continually being made, but the records are scanty, and as writers were few in those days, the town clerk or the monastic scribe had more important matter to set down than that which referred to the making and selling of ordinary rough earthenware porringers, dishes, mugs and cruiskens.

Any chance cargo of ware that happened to find its way to one of these early potters had its influence upon their productions, so that crude attempts were continually being made to imitate in the material available such wares as came from France, the Low Countries, Spain, and perhaps more especially Italy.

A few reasons may be assigned among others as to why domestic table ware was not manufactured or sought after to any extent. The customs of the time

did not require it. The style of cooking was bar-
barous, and articles used as food were limited in
variety. Tea had not taken its place here as a daily
beverage. Its introduction into this country gave
the manufacturer of smaller wares the incentive to
produce articles suitable and necessary to contain it
while brewing and drinking, and to vie with each other
in placing on the market articles of utility and ornament. Before this incentive came it was not that
those who made the pottery then in use could not have
supplied domestic pottery, for the craftsman who
could achieve such masterpieces as we see in the tiles
and ornamental pieces of that time, displaying such
knowledge of clay and glaze, could have diverted their
energies to domestic requirements had any demand
been made upon them.

Again, during the Stuart Period, when civil war was
disturbing the peace and settlement of the potter, it
was obviously no time for him to apply himself to
discovery and experiment in a group of materials that
necessitated, perhaps more than in any other trade,
close application over a prolonged series of trials.

And one may be permitted to suggest that in an age
when swaggering, drinking, and riotous behaviour
were looked upon almost as accomplishments, the more
durable and convenient utensil to emphasise a point in
a drunken quarrel would be a " leather bottel " or a
pewter plate, rather than an earthenware pitcher,
tyg, or platter. '

At the commencement of the seventeenth century
little progress was made ; the small " potworks " were
to a great extent scattered in isolated moorlands, the

produce being carried in panniers on asses' backs to the nearest fair or market. Burslem itself was cut off from the commercial part of the Midlands, it had no turnpike road, and although it was a town, the only one in the Pottery district, it had little direct intercourse with the outer world. In 1740 the general post letters were delivered by an old woman every Sunday from Newcastle-under-Lyme, and in 1750 it only contained five shops, two of which belonged to butchers, so that all shop goods had to be fetched from Newcastle. Twenty years later letters were delivered to Burslem three or four times a week by a man on horseback.

Amusements were of the coarsest kind—bull-baiting, bear-baiting, and cock-fighting—which reached their highest pitch at the Annual Wakes, the celebration of which was a Saturnalia.

Into the midst of these unpromising conditions, as far as the neighbourhood was concerned, Josiah Wedgwood was born in 1730, but he had the advantage of coming from a stock who had long pursued a different course; they were potters of some position and importance in their native town. He was the thirteenth and youngest child of Thomas and Mary Wedgwood, of the Churchyard Works, Burslem, and in the living-house attached he first saw the light. His mother was a delicate, well-educated woman, at whose knee he learnt the rudiments of reading, writing and arithmetic, and there had his first lessons in integrity and character building.

Josiah was a delicate child, and this state of health was more or less with him all his life; at times it completely laid him aside, but his natural trend was to seek after and accumulate knowledge, his active brain at all times quickly assimilating facts and deducing from his observations practical and tangible results. His mental energy was always far in advance of his physical power to perform.

His school education was started at a dame school in Burslem, and continued in a boys' school at New-castle-under-Lyme, where he remained until he was nine years of age, when the head master, a Mr. Blount, considered that he had made good progress in his studies.

At this time his father died, and he was taken from school to start life on the " potworks " with his elder brother, Thomas, as master.

Josiah Wedgwood was honoured by Royal Patronage during the latter part of the eighteenth century, and produced the finest of the early Queensware for use in the palace. Some of these pieces remain to-day, acting as an incentive to our present Queen and forming the nucleus of her private collection. This collection, though comparatively small, has some very interesting examples, which are brought together in a room prepared specially to receive them in Windsor Castle. This room is correctly decorated in the Adam style to Her Majesty's own suggestion, and makes a perfect little Wedgwood Museum. Here are histori-cally interesting items, and others collected by Her Majesty—a true Wedgwood enthusiast, appreciating to the full that technique which gives to this particular branch of the potter's craft its real intrinsic value. But this collection differs in one respect from almost any other : it has beautiful examples of the finest possible execution, wrought specially to the Royal command. This cultured enthusiasm has realised that to encourage highly trained craftsmanship at the present day is the surest way to elevate the taste and educate the capabilities of the worker. The author of these notes has reason to know that this Royal enthusiasm has been productive of a loyal appreciation, resulting in the putting forward of the very best into such tasks as have proved in themselves a reward far in excess of any that can be estimated either by wages or commercial transaction.

Such productions will live, and when time has cast the inevitable halo around them, the collectors of the future will gladly include them among their " choice bits " and reverence the far-seeing taste which caused their preservation to-day. If it had not been for such Royal Patrons as Queen Charlotte and the Empress Catherine of Russia during the eighteenth century, much of the finest pottery would not have survived to this day. (See pp. 85, 232.)

Before closing these introductory remarks, it will be well to inform collectors of Wedgwood Ware that there are facilities for them all to consult the collection of specimens and manuscripts which are to be found in the Etruria Museum upon the old works in Staffordshire, and any genuine inquirer will find that information is willingly given by the curator in charge. Many do not even know of the existence of this museum, and very few have any idea of the mass of detail gathered together there which shows at a glance what a marvellous master of the technical difficulties of pottery manufacture the founder of Etruria was. Every

writer on Wedgwood has extracted from this source,
but the supply is by no means exhausted, and it is not
too much to say that it should be the " Mecca " of
every pilgrim who travels in quest of the gems of
English pottery.

Admission can be obtained any day, free of any
payment, with or without previous appointment, by
applying at the lodge of the Wedgwood Works at
Etruria, Stoke-on-Trent, where those interested are
always welcome.   This may be a useful hint to those
who are, or intend to be, collectors.

II

PRE-ETRUSCAN
WEDGWOOD

CHAPTER II

PRE-ETRUSCAN WEDGWOOD

AT the death of his father, Thomas Wedgwood, the
boy Josiah left school and at the age of nine years was
put to work as a potter in his father's works, which
now had become those of his elder brother, Thomas
Wedgwood.

Here he was put to the bench, and began to learn
the art of " throwing " or making pots upon the wheel
(the most ancient of crafts, the forming of the shape in
the plastic clay upon the revolving, horizontal turn-

table), or as he himself described it, he started " on the bottom rung of the ladder." In 1744 his apprenticeship was decided upon and he became bound to his brother Thomas at the Churchyard Works, " to Learn his Art Mistery Occupation or Imployment of Thrower and Handleing " [1] for five years. A boy who had always lived among potters and potting would naturally take to the trade more readily than a stranger ; accordingly young Josiah was soon able to take an active part in his brother's works, and he was sufficiently capable to apply himself diligently to the improvement of the shapes and sizes of the ordinary ware, the manufacture of which was increasing by leaps and bounds at this period.

Owing to recurring weakness in his right knee, due originally to an illness during his twelfth year, he had to leave the " throwing " wheel at about the age of sixteen. This led him to turn his attention to other branches, the details of which he tackled and mastered in the same accurate and skilful way in which he had applied himself to the potter's wheel, and by persistent experiment in other channels and attention to the improvement of minor details, he became the medium of most important discoveries. This period of his life from youth to early manhood was a time of determined self-culture, when mental and moral character was strongly developed.

Although at this time the general working of a factory had greatly improved, there was need of further system and accuracy. The young apprentice's strong sense of discipline and order could not be repressed.

[1] From Wedgwood's indenture (Hanley Museum).

In the Churchyard Works reforms were to be observed; materials were carefully selected, glazes accurately prepared, standard thicknesses of clay bats for making plates, dishes, and moulded pieces were insisted upon, and accuracy all round was enforced, so that articles of the same pattern could be relied upon as being of similar shape, size, and thickness. These have always been distinguishing characteristics of ware which came from the Wedgwood factories.

His success was so encouraging to himself that at the close of his apprenticeship young Josiah decided to break away from the old home works, and he accepted a partnership with a certain John Harrison, a tradesman of Newcastle-under-Lyme, who had invested money in a "potworks" at Stoke belonging to a potter named Alders. This pottery produced mottled, cloudy, tortoiseshell (glazed with lead ore), and also salt glazed wares. They made tea ware, jugs, and other articles.

As soon as Wedgwood became a partner, improvement was noticed in "body," shape, glaze, and decoration. Harrison became interested, but did not agree with Wedgwood in spending so much time on improvement, suggesting and effecting alterations in the general products which did not immediately realise returns. This disagreement brought the partnership to a rather speedy termination.

Soon after this a new partnership was offered to him, and this time by a worthy man, Thomas Whieldon, who had started a pottery at Fenton Low, in 1740, and had built up a good business from a small foundation.

In many ways he was like Wedgwood : he had a liberal mind, a clear judgment, a love of accuracy and perfection, integrity in business, a genial temper, and benevolence.

He had employed Aaron Wood, a modeller, who had gained some reputation and whose work was being asked for by most of the potters in the neighbourhood.

In 1754, when Wedgwood was twenty-four years old, he entered into this new position. Whieldon had several apprentices, among whom was Josiah Spode, afterwards a famous potter. William Greatbach, who personally, and by his descendants, was connected with Etruria during over a hundred years' service, also worked at one time at Fenton Low.

No record exists of any of the improvements or productions that were the result of this partnership, but it is correct to assume that as the relations lasted for five years, they were very amicable. Only one notebook of Whieldon's remains, which is preserved at the Corporation Museum at Hanley, Stoke-on-Trent, and contains mainly mixing notes and particulars as to hiring and wages, but the Experiment Book in Etruria Museum, in handwriting, exquisitely neat and free from alterations, tells conclusively the method and business ability of Wedgwood and throws an interesting light upon the closing part of those years. Here he says in a sort of explanatory preface :—

" This suite of experiments was begun at Fenton " hall, in the parish of Stoke upon Trent, about the " beginning of the year 1759, in my partnership with

" Mr. Whieldon, for the improvement of our manufac-
" ture of earthenware, which at that time stood in
" great need of it, the demand for our goods decreasing
" daily, and the trade universally complained of as
" being bad & in a declining condition.

" White Stone ware " (viz. with Salt glaze) was the
" principal article of our manufacture. But this had
" been made a long time, and the prices were now
" reduced so low, that the potters could not afford to
" bestow much expence upon it, or to make it so good
" in any respect as the ware would otherwise admit of.——
" And with regard to Elegance of form, that was an
" object very little attended to.

" The article next in consequence to the Stoneware
" was an imitation of Tortoiseshell. But as no im-
" provement had been made in this branch for several
" years, the country was grown weary of it ; and
" though the price had been lowered from time to time,
" in order to increase the sale, the expedient did not
" answer, and something new was wanted, to give a
" little spirit to the business.

" I had already made an imitation of Agate ; which
" was esteemed beautiful & a considerable improve-
" ment ; but people were surfeited with wares of these
" variegated colors. These considerations induced me
" to try for some more solid improvement, as well in
" the *Body*, as the *Glazes*, the *Colours*, & the *Forms*,
" of the articles of our manufacture.

" I saw the field was spacious, and the soil so good,
" as to promise an ample recompence to any one who
" should labour diligently in its cultivation." [1]

[1] From Experiment Book (Etruria Museum).

Then follows a careful description of the method in which he catalogues and marks his trials, and as many of his experimental pieces have found their way outside into private and other collections, it will be interesting to add these further extracts from the preface :—

" The degrees of heat, in my former books were " expressed by the different ovens, & the different parts " of them, which the experiment-pieces had been fired " in. G O signified the gloss oven, B O the Biscuit " oven, and W O the white oven ; and the letters " B, M, T, prefixed to these meant the bottom, middle, " & top of the respective ovens — T B O means the " highest part of the Biscuit oven in which we set " ware, which is below the top of the chimneys or " flues, called bags by the potters ; and T T B O " signifies the uppermost sagar of the pile, except the " one with which it is covered." (See illustration Chapter VIII, facing p. 205.)

" The experiments being here set down & numbered " in the order they were made, and many of them " having been resumed & further prosecuted after the " intervention of several others ; it has been found " necessary, to arrange the whole into classes and " sections — A small column on the right hand of the " page of this book refers to the class and section, " the number of dots · — : — : signifying the first, " second, & third class ; and the figure following these " dots, the section of that class." [1]

[1] From Experiment Book (Etruria Museum).

It may be well just here to clear up a little of the uncertainty which surrounds this period of the manufacture of ware which has generally received the name Whieldon, not admittedly because it is thought by connoisseurs to have issued from his factory, but for the reason that it marks and belongs to an epoch.

Whieldon could not have made much, if any, " Cauliflower " and " Pineapple " ware at the time Wedgwood was in partnership, nor is it likely that he made much progress after the initiative and research of his young partner had been withdrawn.

We make the first statement with assurance, for upon referring to the Experiment Book quoted from, the following entry gives a firm foundation to rest upon. The seventh experiment or trial entered upon the first page is :—

" 7.
$$\frac{3}{120} \left| \frac{17}{30} \right| \frac{33}{9}$$
A Green glaze, to be laid on Common white (or cream color) biscuit ware. Very good—March 23, 1759." [1]

The numbers above the line are in red, and indicate the materials used, the numbers below being in black, and refer to the quantities of each used in the mixture.

" This N[o.] is the result of many Expts. which I
" made in order to introduce a new species of colored
" ware, to be fired along with the tortoiseshell & Agate
" wares in our common gloss ovens. —

" This N[o.] has been used several years very success-
" fully, in a great variety of articles both for home and
" foreign consumption." [2]

[1] From Experiment Book (Etruria Museum).   [2] *Ibid.*

As Wedgwood's partnership agreement with Whieldon came to an end early in 1759, it is certain that the green glaze so much prized and always attached to Whieldon's name could not have been in use at Fenton Low before, and as " Cauliflower " and " Pineapple " ware were not produced without it, we have a fairly conclusive proof that it was one of the chief factors which helped Wedgwood to the decision to start manufacturing on his own account, which he did when he had made arrangements to rent the Ivy House and Works at Burslem.

Further, when in 1905 the moulds, blocks and trials, which had lain hidden for so many years at Etruria, were rediscovered, among them were the salt glazed pattern block moulds of the " Cauliflower " and " Pineapple " pieces,[1] besides others of the early Burslem period, and it is not likely that these were brought away from Fenton Low, as Wedgwood would scarcely have part ownership in such material along with partnership. Therefore one can say almost decidedly that these wares were " Wedgwood " as far as invention and design were concerned, although undoubtedly copied by many, probably by Whieldon among the number, after the dissolution of partnership. The general marking of ware was not the practice, and the difficulty of placing pieces to the credit of any one manufacturer will always exist.

It was in the early part of 1759, probably April, that Wedgwood severed his business connection with Whieldon and decided to try his fortune as a manufacturer.

[1] See illus. facing p. 65.

THE IVY HOUSE WORKS, BURSLEM.

(*From an old oil painting.*)

THE BRICK HOUSE WORKS, BURSLEM.

(*From an old woodcut.*)

(Etruria Museum.)

[*To face page* 64.

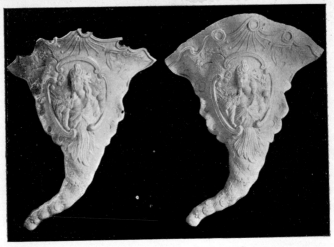

SALT GLAZE BLOCK MOULDS.

1. SALT GLAZED PIECE FROM THE MOULD NO. 2.
2. BLOCK MOULD OF CORNUCOPIA.
3. BLOCK MOULD FOR " LANDSCAPE " TEAPOT.
4. BLOCK MOULD FOR " PINEAPPLE " SAUCE BOAT.
5. BLOCK MOULD FOR " CAULIFLOWER " TEAPOT.

(Etruria Museum.)

[*To face page* 65.

Beside the actual practical knowledge he had obtained of the potter's craft during his apprenticeship years and the two partnerships which followed, he was undoubtedly well equipped for such a venture. His research among materials and their chemical properties, the careful deductions which he had systematically made, of which he has left abundant proof in his recorded later triumphs, his appreciation of all natural things, and his ability to make use of what his keen intellect observed, gave him the courage of this conviction. The opportunities for the industry in the future were very promising if only he could make use of that material which his foresight led him to believe existed in his everyday surroundings. As he had applied himself to self-training in a variety of subjects, thereby fitting himself to take the position of master, he was able to undertake the education of any promising lad or workman who presented himself.

Many interesting anecdotes are handed down relating to his daily habits and pursuits after knowledge during boyhood and as a young man—how he made collections of natural objects and studied closely any drawing, painting, or print which came into his hands—but in the absence of any actual proof in the form of document, we cannot say more than that the greatest proof of the truth of such tales is present in the result shown in the taste and excellence of all to which he put his hands, qualities that showed no backward turn as his life went on, but increased a hundredfold until they permeated the whole atmosphere of his works and continued to be the main incentive in the manufacture which has stood the test of more than a hundred years since his death and are still a potent force to-day and the envy and admiration of potters all the world over.

The first start was naturally in a modest way, but one of his first arrangements was to secure the help of his cousin, Thomas Wedgwood, and as the document recording this arrangement is dated December 1758 and comes into force in the following May, it gives a further clue as to the actual time at which he was starting his factory in Burslem. The Agreement reads :—

" Decr 30th 1758—Memorand^m of an Agreement " between Josiah Wedgwood of the Parish of Stoke in " the County of Stafford, Potter, and Thos Wedgwood " Journeyman now liveing at the City of Worster " potter, the s^d Thos Wedgwood engageth to serve " the s^d Josiah Wedgwood as a Journeyman from the " first of May 1759 to the 11 of Novemb^r 1765 and is " to receive of the s^d Josiah Wedgwood twenty two " Pounds of lawfull money for every years service." [1]

Wedgwood's capital was at first limited, and until it increased it would be impossible for him to spread his wings for flight into the larger sphere whither his ambitions and hopes lured him ; he could not for some time extend his trade by employing a large number of workmen to augment his output, nor introduce new wares which no doubt at this time he had already conceived in his own fertile brain, but we know by later revelations that he exercised sound judgment in choice of workmen, where possible, as lifelong service is recorded in some cases.

[1] Wedgwood manuscript (Etruria Museum).

1.   2.

1. " CAULIFLOWER " TEA CADDY.
2. " CAULIFLOWER " TEAPOT.

(British Museum.)

3.   4.

3. " PINEAPPLE " TEAPOT.
4. " PINEAPPLE " TEA CADDY.

(Wedgwood Institute, Burslem.)

[To face page 66.

TEAPOT, " LANDSCAPE " PATTERN.

TEAPOT, " MARBLED."
(*Marked Wedgwood & Bentley.*)
(British Museum.)

[*To face page* 67.

At this time the methods of working in general use in the Potteries were slovenly, and to improve and educate his workmen must have been his foremost thought ; his personal attention to every detail is not a matter of conjecture, as the comparatively few pieces that exist of this period show the greatest attention to details of technique. Owing to the shortage of assistance he would himself be responsible for all of the work which was not embraced by the potter, or actual maker of the ware ; thus the designing of shapes and models would in a great measure fall to him, all the office work and that of the warehouse too.

Actual records, and books, if he had time to make and keep them, have not come down to us to help in registering the progress made at this early period, but it is fairly safe to say that business must have been very considerable, for we find references in his early letters to the excursions he was making into fresh fields of experiment.

As early as 1763 [1] he had installed an " engine turning " lathe upon his works and was producing red ware (called then Red China because of its vitreous character and similarity to the imported red ware from China), decorated with patterns produced by this means. In 1764 he sends a sample of this to his friend Bentley, writing : " having been extreme busy on many " acc[ts], have sent you a sample of one hobby horse " (Engine turning)—this branch hath cost me a great " deal of time and thought, and must cost me more." [2] That he afterwards turned this to good account is shown

[1] Commonplace book (Etruria Museum).
[2] Letter, Wedgwood to Bentley, May 28, 1764.

when during the next year he writes to his nephew Byerley, who is in London, telling him to show certain new patterns and saying : " if you have got ord^{rs} from six shops for these articles it is enough at present, only I sho^d be glad to have my customers see them or they may be affronted as they were at not being shown the Engin'^{d} T. pots. I mean good China Shops for I wo^d not put them into any others." [1]

In the same month he writes to his brother John in London, asking him to see Sir Wm. Meredith :—

" I wish he wo^d give me a copper plate with his
" Arms suitable for Table plates & a Crest (if he wo^d
" like it) to fill up one of the compartm^{ts} in the dish
" rims, it wo^d then be in my power to present him with
" one of the completest services of Staffordshire Ware,
" ever got up in the County & I sho^d be glad if you
" wo^d tell him so much." [2]

In the same letter he goes on to say :—

" Our London order and some foreign ones just
" come to hand are very large, & require my constant
" attention in ordering & seeing got up &c &c.
" . . . I do not want any more ord^{rs} unless for
" collyflower ware." [3]

This all suggests an overflow of work which must have tried his somewhat limited resources to the utmost at this time, but it shows also that he had launched out into other wares, and his desire to present

[1] Wedgwood to Byerley, February 11, 1765.
[2] Wedgwood letter to John Wedgwood, February 13, 1765 (Etruria Museum). [3] Ibid.

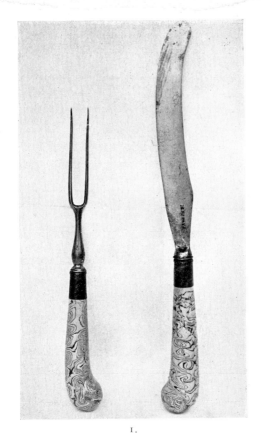

I.

1. KNIFE AND FORK, AGATE WARE HANDLES.
(British Museum.)

2.   3.

2. TEAPOT IN RED BODY, ENGINE-TURNED.
(Burslem Institute.)

3. COVER, RED BODY, " CRABSTOCK " PATTERN.
(Etruria Museum.)

[To face page 68.

I.

I. CREAM COLOUR VASE, RELIEF AND ENGINE
TURNED, BURSLEM PERIOD.

2.

3.

2. VASE. IMITATION OF PORPHYRY, ON MARBLE PLINTH.
3. FLOWER VASE, IMITATION OF PORPHYRY.

(Etruria Museum.)

[To face page 69.

a complete service of Table Ware to so distinguished a person as Sir William shows a confidence and ability to fulfil it. Still all this does not repress his insatiable thirst for experiment in fresh fields.

" I am going," he says, " to be very busy, haveing
" come to a full resolution of attempting in earnest
" the French Ware, & am every night forming schemes
" for that purpose, I mention nights for whilst Tom [1]
" is from home I am too closely confind to the Counting
" house to do anything of that sort in the day." [2]

During this year (1765) his first visions of extending his borders are formulating—Etruria, shapeless yet tangible, begins to hold a place in his considerations. " I do not intend to make this ware " (referring to the French White Ware) " at Burslem & am therefore " laying out for an agreeable and convenient situation " elsewhere." [3]

Sir William Meredith was at this time a truly useful patron who " heaped favours " upon him so abundantly that his " heart is overflowing with sentiments of " gratitude and thankfullness for y^r goodness for " lead^g me into improvem^{ts}," and he continues his letter by saying that such inducements to industry demand his utmost attention ; if he does not outstrip his fellows, the fault must be owing to a great want of genius or application.

During all this close attention to business he still finds time to throw himself heart and soul into the new scheme for inland navigation, and his connections and

---

[1] His nephew Byerley.
[2] Wedgwood letter to John Wedgwood, February 16, 1765.
[3] Letter to John Wedgwood, March 6, 1765.

" things—& have him in y^r Room that he may be
" und^r your Eye." [1]

This gives some idea of the persistent energy which
resulted in the output of the much-coveted table ware
that was becoming the talk of all and the fashion to
procure. Much of this is still existing, so that the
collector need not despair ; pieces may be discovered
in out-of-the-way hiding-places, and every year reveals
some fresh unknown treasure.

The invention of the method of printing on pottery
had been made probably as early as 1752, at first by
John Sadler, a printer of Liverpool, who afterwards
took Guy Green into partnership. Their process was
patented about 1754 and had thus been in use for some
five years before Wedgwood started in business, but
with the improvement of his Queensware came the
desire to utilise this most satisfactory and ready method
of decoration. It is therefore highly probable that at
the very earliest opportunity he availed himself of this
invention and soon brought his own individuality to
bear upon it in the form of design applied to his
requirements. Great quantities of the " white ware "
from Burslem were sent to Sadler & Green at Liverpool
to be printed, fired, and returned, for at the date of
the first available record we find that an invoice for
over £64 is sent to Wedgwood which represents the
cost of printing and firing 1,730 pieces of ware, which
are specified as : Teapots in three sizes, Mugs in two
sizes, Bowls, all sizes, Coffee pots, Sugars, Cream
Ewers, and Cups & Saucers. This invoice is dated
April 11, 1764.

[1] Wedgwood's letters (Etruria Museum).

The business of Sadler & Green must have been fairly extensive, for earlier in the same year they write to Wedgwood asking for payment :—

" We expect a Remittance very soon ; for I assure
" you we have not known the Want of Cash so much as
" at present this long time.   We have paid 350£ for
" Plates " (copper engraved plates) " for the Cream
" Colour only, which is considerably more than the
" cash we have had from you & what ware we have
" sold here ; besides our Labour, fire, Wages, &c." [1]

Although it is not likely at all that the whole amount or anything like it was at the time spent in engraving for Wedgwood patterns, it serves to show that the little Works at Ivy House had very decidedly adopted this process and was using it with some enthusiasm. Messrs. Sadler & Green procured ware from all sources, and many potters must have supplied them with the articles necessary for their own orders.   Wedgwood supplied an increasing demand for his Queensware through this channel ; with every invoice charging for printing and firing came an order for various items of ware, generally couched in urgent terms.   The first order that remains is dated Oct. 19, 1764, and reads :—

" I write now to desire you'll send us a parcel of
" Quart & Pint Mugs —   We lost the sale this Day of
" 8 Doz Mason Quarts, not having one to sell, nor one
" Plain.   We have not so many Basons neither as you
" have ordered—nor Coffee Pots —   We are very low
" indeed." [2]

[1] Wedgwood Invoices, January 1, 1764 (Etruria Museum).
[2] Sadler & Green's correspondence (Etruria Museum).

There is a great gap in correspondence, manuscripts, etc., after this, which may be accounted for by the two removals. In 1764 the Brick House Works were taken and the workpeople removed there. This factory was afterwards known as the Bell House Works, as it was the first factory in the Potteries to have a belfry and bell added, to ring the potters to work instead of calling them together by blowing a horn. The second and final move to the new works at Etruria was made in 1769.

It is quite probable that papers may have been lost, gone astray, or destroyed; yet the connections with Sadler & Green must have been on the increase all through these years, as the existing invoices for the year 1771—which represent every month in the year—show an amount due for printing and firing of over £650, and a contra account almost as large for ware supplied to Liverpool for their orders.

That the Liverpool printers experienced difficulties in their work is shown by the two following extracts, which direct information will not be uninteresting to collectors :—

" The very slow Method we have of firing large
" Ware makes it very desirable to find out a more
" expeditious and safe Way, as we have sometimes
" great losses in breakage. If Mr. Wedgwood would
" please to give us his thoughts on the above, we are
" certain his long experience in these Matters would
" enable us to attain this sooner than we could with
" a great deal of trouble and expence." [1]

[1] Sadler & Green's correspondence, May 2, 1771 (Etruria Museum).

1. PEDESTAL, CREAM COLOUR, ENGINE-TURNED.
2. VASE, CREAM COLOUR, WITH RELIEF DECORATION.
3. PEDESTAL, CREAM COLOUR, ENGINE-TURNED.

4. COVERED VASE, TWO-HANDLED, CREAM COLOUR, ENGINE-TURNED.
5. GLACIÈRE, CREAM COLOUR, RELIEF DECORATION AND PIERCED BORDERS.
6. VASE. CREAM COLOUR, FLUTED AND RUNNER DECORATION.

(Etruria Museum.)

[To face page 74.

1. VASE, AGATE WARE, SURFACE DECORATION.   2. VASE, AGATE WARE, SOLID BODY.
3. VASE, AGATE WARE, SURFACE DECORATION.

All on white jasper plinths.

" We have often observed that those pieces that
" have stood long in the Warehouse are most subject to
" this Misfortune (blistering) in firing ; and therefore
" beg Mr. Wedgwood will give *strict Orders* that no
" plates, Dishes, &c. be sent here but such as have
" been lately fired, and that they be pack'd in dry
" straw, &c." [1]

Of the other articles, spoons, knife hafts, and small
ware which were part of the output from the Burslem
Works, very little remains ; the pieces generally obtainable are the pistol-shaped knife and fork handles, and
these were made in various patterns of Agate Ware,
different coloured clays mingled together to form an
imitation of natural stones.

From this beginning, which was the result of his
early experiments in staining clays with metallic
oxides, he was afterwards successful in introducing his
Marbled, Agate, and Onyx Vases, which gave him such
a rich field to work upon when he started at Etruria.

Little has been said about the " Cauliflower,"
" Pineapple," " Cabbage," and " Landscape " ware of
his early days, but there is not much to say ; he
certainly produced this plentifully, but when the
public began to be surfeited with it, and other makes
flooded the market, his energy led him on to perfect
and introduce his other wares, which he apparently
did with great success, leaving his competitors behind ;
and so we pass on from this difficult early period, so
scantily furnished with the firm foundation of recorded
facts, to the more certain area embracing the years
commencing with the opening of Etruria in 1769.

[1] Sadler & Green's correspondence, June 6, 1771 (Etruria Museum).

III

CREAM
COLOUR
WARE

CHAPTER III

CREAM COLOUR WARE

Wedgwood's desire to produce cream colour ware—How it came into being—His concentration upon it—Many failures—Success—Perfection of production—Queensware the invention of Wedgwood—Richard Champion's patent—Remarks upon it by Wedgwood—Champion's reply—Further remarks—The early days of Queensware —The old shapes—The earliest dinner ware—Great variety of patterns—Tea ware—Its use for the surgery, kitchen, pantry, bedroom, boudoir, stable and garden— Tiles—The freehand painted decorations upon Queensware—A Staffordshire production—Utensils and accessories—The jelly mould—Elaborate pieces—Decorative useful table ware—The " Russian " service—Interesting articles in the original catalogue—The work of Emile Lessore and Thomas Allen.

CREAM COLOUR, as the name of a special body, is so universally known that very few users of it ever stop to inquire as to how it first came into existence, and some there are still who would not consider that its birth and baptism, so to speak, had any connection with " Wedgwood " Ware, yet his energies were largely concentrated upon this vast area of useful ware, for in the desire to serve his day and generation he made articles to furnish every possible domestic requirement where pottery was capable of filling it, besides supplying a great number of commercial and scientific needs where the material was satisfactory, in many cases proving superior to that which it superseded.

Thus we find it not only upon the tables of our houses, but in the kitchens and storerooms ; in decorative pieces of exquisite technique on the mantelshelves, and in the cabinets of the drawing-rooms and boudoirs of our large mansions and humble homes. Chemical laboratories and photographic and artists' studios use it, it has proved itself absolutely necessary to the electrician, and sanitary science has made great use of it. In each and all of these branches are some pieces which prove of interest to the collector, for Cream Colour has always been an excellent medium for the expression of form and colour, use sooner or later suggesting decoration.

How did " Cream Colour " first come into being ? The earliest attempt to whiten the ware was by the mixture of flint with the lead ore to form the glaze, but this can in no way be called a " body " colour. A White or Cream Coloured clay had been known and used during the seventeenth century, but was only employed as a material in which to make ornaments from a mould and apply them on to the red or buff coloured marl, in the form of relief decoration. The son of Astbury [1] is accredited with making the first cream coloured ware, when about 1725 he mixed marl and flint, at a later date carefully preparing and blending the finest native clay and flint.

This was again improved by Aaron Wedgwood, and Enoch Booth of Tunstall, the latter the first potter who fired his ware twice, that is, first in an oven to bring it to a biscuit state, and then, after dipping it in liquid glaze, in a second oven.

[1] The potter.

It was not until Wedgwood had settled in the Ivy House Works that he concentrated all his energies for a period upon Cream Colour only ; every essential detail was the object of his care. His patience was often tried, repeated failures were disheartening, but his amazing persistence in the face of all drawbacks was finally rewarded by complete success, which came more rapidly than he himself had anticipated.

There is a difference, difficult—one may almost say impossible—to describe, between the productions of Josiah Wedgwood and those of his predecessors or even his contemporaries. He seemed to work on so large a scale and in such a style as to harmonise completely with the materials that he had improved and fashioned for his own use. The delicacy and finish of his wares induced many imitators to follow, but they were not happy in their results, they did not arrive at the same perfection, and this can be said as truthfully in regard to his " useful " and " table " ware as of his choice ornamental pieces ; indeed, his monument would stand if it had been erected upon no other achievement than his Cream Colour, for it influenced the whole subsequent manufacture of pottery in England. The " potting " was so good in every detail, every part was in complete accord with its neighbour in a service— plates " nested," lids fitted, spouts and lips poured, and handles performed their function, forms were adapted to their uses—and with all this the artistic character was never missing. This is a great claim to make, but it is fearlessly advanced as the greatest of all the factors that resulted in success.

It is indeed a question if Cream Colour ware really

existed in the form that we to-day recognise it, before Wedgwood had created it ; certainly as " Queensware " it was his invention, and that is what every lover of earthenware wants : the " body " must be there, the glaze, the technique ; and it was these things that were " Wedgwood " and have remained the head line for all since to copy. But this, after all, is undisputed, and his " Queensware " was the agent that created the demand for Staffordshire Cream Coloured ware throughout the world.

When Richard Champion of Bristol applied to Parliament for an extension of the term of his patent right for the sole use of certain materials for making porcelain, the petition was referred to a Select Committee of the House. As soon as this was done Wedgwood, in the interest of the potters, presented a " Memorial " giving the reasons in full why such an extension would be injurious to the industry generally. To this, Champion made a " Reply " at some length, which again called forth further " Remarks " from Wedgwood ; those which touched upon Queensware may be repeated here. In these he states that he :—

" . . . is so fully convinced of the great injury that " would be done to the landed, manufacturing, and " commercial interests of this nation by extending the " term of Mr. Champion's monopoly of raw materials, " of which there are immense quantities in the King-" dom, and confining the use of them to one or a few " hands . . . he thinks that himself and all manu-" facturers should be protected in the *free use* of all " raw materials that are not invented by men, but are

" the natural productions of the earth. When Mr.
" Wedgwood discovered the art of making *Queensware*,
" which employs ten times more people than all the
" China works in the Kingdom, he did not ask for a
" patent for this important discovery. A patent
" would greatly have limited its public utility. Instead
" of *one hundred manufactories* of Queensware there
" would have been *one*, and instead of an exportation
" to all parts of the World, a few pretty things would
" have been made for the amusement of the people
" of fashion in England." [1]

Of the early days of Queensware we have to admit
very little is known, for no records exist, and as our
expressed intention is to assume nothing, the skeleton
of fact that remains is all that can be offered. The
earliest " drawing book " referring to Queensware
contains a collection of shapes numbered from 1 to
1680, and is undated, but the water-mark in the paper
is 1802, which gives the date of the making of this
record. As it begins with number 1, it is fair to
conclude that it is the first form that was made for
reference and includes the shapes which had been
made from the beginning, except the early Burslem
pieces, for no list or illustrations appear to have been
kept of them, and this, it seems, is the correct conclusion to arrive at, as no list at all exists of the
" Cauliflower " and " Pineapple " ware, which was
undoubtedly the early Burslem product.

The index is arranged alphabetically, showing 105

[1] " Remarks upon Mr. Champion's Reply to Mr. Wedgwood's
Memorial on behalf of himself and the Potters in Staffordshire."

different classes of article, and as each article would be produced in fifty different shapes, some idea can be formed of the mass and variety of useful ware that was made in this material, some perfectly plain in outline, others enriched with embossment, and all at times for special orders decorated with bands and lines and painted ornament in hundreds of ways. Many were very ornate, used as centre or side pieces for table decoration, such as the " Pineapple Centre," " Pierced Fruit Bowl," or Baskets, Dessert Dishes, Glacières and Sucriers,[1] and a list which it would tire the reader to wander through ; but all these mentioned are objects which in shape and decoration are essentially collectors' pieces and the variety is so great that in these days it is quite a rare occurrence to come upon two alike, except where whole services have been preserved in families that have possessed them from the day of their original manufacture. Just a short reference may not be out of place and will assist those on the look-out to realise what unexpected " finds " may reward their search. In ordinary service ware the plates were represented by only nine shapes ;[2] this is accounted for by the fact that plates were interchangeable and one shape was used for a number of services. It was the " covered " pieces (soup tureens and vegetable dishes) which gave the distinctive name or style to the service.

The earliest of these plate patterns was undoubtedly the " Queen's Pattern." The " Royal Pattern " was adapted from it, and was used for the service made for

[1] See illus. facing p. 94, etc.
[2] See illus. facing p. 84.

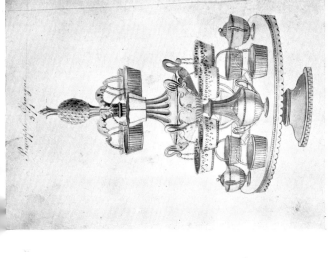

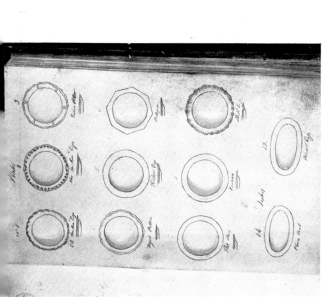

ORIGINAL DRAWINGS FROM OLD PATTERN BOOK.

1. THE FIRST NINE PLATE SHAPES.
2. THE "PINEAPPLE" CENTREPIECE.

(Etruria Museum.)

To face page 84.

1.   2.

1. PLATE, QUEENSWARE, CONCAVE SHAPE, ETRUSCAN BORDER AND
CENTRE SUBJECT IN RED AND BLACK.

2. PLATE, QUEENSWARE, FLAT RIM SHAPE, HAND-PAINTED BORDER
AND SUBJECT.

(Etruria Museum.)

3.   4.

3. PLATE, QUEENSWARE, ROYAL SHAPE, FROM THE "RUSSIAN
SERVICE."

(Liverpool Museum.)

4. PLATE, QUEENSWARE, QUEEN'S SHAPE, PRINTED IN LIVERPOOL
BY SADLER & GREEN.

(Etruria Museum.)

[To face page 85.

Queen Catherine II of Russia. Both these patterns were a survival of the prevailing design generally found in the salt glazed ware plates whose rim panels were stippled or patterned with diaper or pineapple texture surfaces. The "Shell Edge" or "Marine Border"[1] was also one of the earliest patterns, and it was not until a later date that the "Flat Rim" and "Concave Rim"[2] followed, these being adaptations of the old pewter plate shapes.

"I have often been applyd to by Persons of the first "taste to make Table Plates & dishes without any "sharp edge. . . . These would do finely for printing "or painting, I could soon have them model'd . . . & "I think they would not look amiss even plain, but "of this your opinion will determine me."[3]

Dishes of various sizes were made to match the plates. The "covered pieces"—tureens and vegetable dishes—were always of good outline, and the Soup "Terrine" was generally a noble piece. Of these there are no less than forty shapes shown, testifying to the variety of taste catered for.

The comprehensive collection shows also fifty-seven shapes of vegetable dishes (called cover-dishes), sixty-eight sauce tureens, thirty-seven salad bowls, and twenty-seven fruit baskets and stands for dessert, and a most dainty array of "salts," forty in number; some of these are the most beautiful little ornamental pieces, many on stands, or three feet, several in twin

[1] See illus. facing p. 84.
[2] See illus. facing p. 84.
[3] Letter, Wedgwood to Bentley, November 11, 1771.

6

form having twisted handles connecting them, forming charming examples of workmanship apart from the use for which they were intended. The tea-table is represented by twenty-eight teacups and saucers, fifteen coffee cups and saucers, twelve chocolate cups and saucers, and fifty-four butter tubs, every one different in shape and design, yet each exquisitely adapted to its use. Teapots are shown with their accompanying sugar boxes and creams in forty shapes, and when these plain examples are multiplied by the almost endless variety of decorated ones in both relief work and painted pattern, it can be easily imagined why the supply has not yet been exhausted, for good work always found someone appreciative enough to preserve it from harm or destruction, and sound pottery will stand the test of fair wear and tear, and careful usage.

In the hands of Wedgwood, Queensware was called into use for articles which amounted to invention in his day, some of which have been copied and diverted into other materials, in some cases for cheapness, and in others to avoid the chipping and breakage which comes from careless handling, for metal deals kindly with such by denting or bending, but even the best pottery will not withstand the rough usage which it unfortunately too often receives from the average domestic during the process of " washing up."

Looking through the list from this point of view, it is somewhat of a surprise to find the great number of articles which were made for out-of-the-way purposes, not usually connected with the popular idea of the appropriateness of pottery. The ingenious way in which this clean-looking, easily washed, material was utilised for every purpose to which it could be adapted is shown in a complete range of medical utensils— sick feeders, syphons, infusion pots, inhalers, lamps, food warmers and cordial cups, leech pots, spitting pots, bubby pots, as well as a range of sick-chamber ware, an equally complete array for the still-room, pantry, and all culinary purposes, the accessories for the writing table, the toilet table, the boudoir, the bedroom, the stable and the garden.

One of the first uses that Queensware was put to was the making of tiles for lining the walls of bath-rooms. Nothing seems to be forgotten : a glance through this old " drawing book " gives one the feeling that every avenue had been explored and every detail considered.

Most of these old pieces, absolutely plain though they are, are worthy of a place in the cabinet of the collector because of their beauty of outline and the handicraft which they display.

Naturally the desire for decoration was developed with the birth of the form, and in every case where the article was destined to a position where it performed the double duty of being useful and ornamental, some form of painting and colour immediately suggested itself. It is just here that an interesting development took place—a form of decoration which is distinctly English and the direct outcome of the Staffordshire Pottery designer is to be observed in the very dainty and beautifully executed freehand painted borders and sprays which occur on Queensware that was made and sent out from the Potteries at the latter part of the eighteenth and early nineteenth centuries. The evolution was in this way : When Sir William Hamilton introduced into this country the treasures of Etruscan Art, Wedgwood was among the first who was influenced by them. The pure outline and classic form was reflected in the shapes of his vases, flowerpots, tureens and cover-dishes, and the simple borders of ivy leaf and berry, the Greek Fret, and the adaptation of the " Egg and Tongue " [1] that occur upon these old vases, were at first painted in narrow bands upon the rims and edges of the Queensware. These afterwards became a little more elaborated. Under the keen master potter, aided and encouraged by the taste of his wealthy patrons and customers, the native artistry of the painter began to have free play, and from his own garden his nature study found expression in the very beautifully conventionalised floral borders and bands which are so admirably adapted to the texture and colour of the Queensware. Many of the patterns were the direct suggestion and design of some special patron who ordered a service and required it to be carried out to his own drawing.

When the refining and limiting classic feeling was on the wane, the floral painting began to overstep its legitimate area, and lost its quality of design, becoming mere imitation of nature which soon usurped the whole surface, and the " pot " became merely the canvas on which to display clever ceramic painting, which reached its climax during the early Victorian Era.

But this truly Staffordshire production, which was, of course, soon dispersed by travelling and migrating

[1] See illus. facing p. 88.

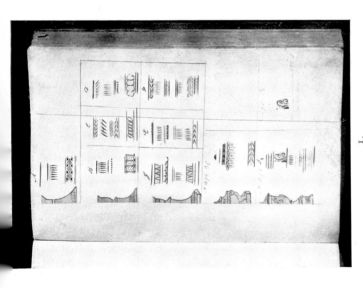

I.

2.

TWO PAGES OF THE OLD PATTERN BOOK, SHOWING DECORATION OF PIECES (1), AND PLATE BORDERS (2).

[To face page 88.

I.   2.   3.

4.   5.   6.

7.   8.   9.

HAND-PAINTED QUEENSWARE.

1 & 3. CUSTARD CUPS.   2. COVERED SUGAR.
4 & 6. CANDLESTICKS.   5. TEAPOT.

(Etruria Museum.)

7, 8 & 9 THREE FLOWER VASES, QUEENSWARE, FLUTED
AND RUNNER DECORATION.

(Wedgwood Institute, Burslem.)

[To face page 89.

pottery painters wherever pots were being made, marks a definite epoch in the evolution of English pottery and is sufficiently confined in its purity of application to one period, thus forming in itself an interesting field of operation for the collector.

Among the side lines, as it were, of the services were included such furnishings for the pieces as drainers, dish tilters, knife supports, spoons, ladles, and fish "trowels";[1] these all received some decoration to match with the pattern on the larger pieces, and a good specimen is shown in the illustration of a fish trowel,[1] that even in the black and white reproduction gives some idea of the balance and finish of the whole, with its delicate piercing and neat painted pattern in green and brown.

Utilitarian ware was always a very strong feature in the cream coloured product and the oft-expressed idea so fully carried out in actual practice, that a piece of ornamental ware should be of some use, and the reverse that useful ware should be ornamental, is seen to advantage in the great number of articles which were made for ordinary household use, where the form and finish of kitchen ware was so carefully studied.

Among this class is to be found still in some old houses the dairy ware which has been in use for over one hundred years, the beautiful and finely proportioned cream steins and settling pans ; some are quite plain but others received very nicely freehand painted border patterns in monochrome or colour. It is interesting to record that among such carefully used vessels our Queen has some pieces of such utilitarian

[1] See illus. facing p. 91.

ware which were made originally for Queen Charlotte, the wife of George III, and which have been in use, probably, in a dairy. These pieces have an " ivy wreath border " in colour.

Another interesting adaptation is the jelly mould. (See illus. facing p. 91.) The mould proper is in plain Cream Colour just fluted on the inside ; into this was poured the warm transparent jelly, sufficient to fill the mould when the square obelisk was dropped down into it. Holes, four in number, at the base of this obelisk, were made to allow any overflow of jelly, which was then allowed to cool in the usual way ; when this was complete the mould and its contents were inverted and the outside mould taken off, leaving the jelly as a thick transparent casing to the inner obelisk, which was now placed upon a dish and served up as a decoration to the table, as the flower painting underneath gave the jelly a rich ornamental effect. Several of these decorated interiors have survived and appear in cabinets, but we have only seen two complete jelly moulds of this sort, one being that illustrated here.   (See illus. facing p. 91.) As far as we know, this idea has never been utilised in any other material, and some who possess the obelisk half of the mould have wondered what its use could have been.

Some very elaborate centre pieces and epergnes were also made, perhaps the richest in effect being the " Pineapple Centre." A complete one is not known to exist now, but when fully dressed with all its hanging baskets containing fruits, sweetmeats, and flowers, it must have made a very rich decoration for the centre of a well-dressed table.   As this is such an interesting

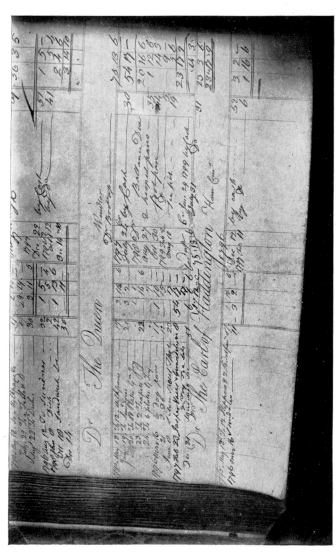

PART OF A PAGE FROM THE OLD LEDGER, SHOWING THE MILK PANS REFERRED TO ON PAGE 232.

(Etruria Museum.)

[To face page 90.

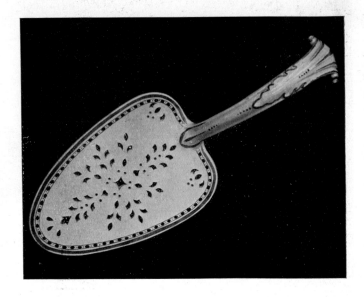

FISH TROWEL, QUEENSWARE, HAND-PAINTED.
(Victoria and Albert Museum.)

JELLY MOULD, QUEENSWARE, HAND-PAINTED.
(Etruria Museum.)

[To face Punch Glass Stand and Chestnut Bowl.

PUNCH GLASS STAND, QUEENSWARE, PIERCED AND RUNNER
DECORATION.

(Victoria and Albert Museum.)

CHESTNUT BOWL, QUEENSWARE, PERFORATED COVER.

(Etruria Museum.)

[*To face Fish Trowel and Jelly Mound.*

SOUP TUREEN AND STAND, QUEENSWARE, IMPERIAL SHAPE, HAND-PAINTED.

DISH, QUEENSWARE, ROYAL SHAPE, HAND-PAINTED.

(Etruria Museum.)

[To face page 91.

and possibly now a non-existent piece, it has been thought that an illustration [1] showing what the original intention of it was, might prove of some service, as parts which have gone astray from their first position may find their way back again.

Of dessert baskets, comports, compotiers, custard stands and cups, and candlesticks, there are a great number which were sent out just in plain glazed cream colour, or with painted decoration, and in this class it is difficult to compute the immense amount and variety that must have been made during the period when these Queensware services were the " fashion " and every lady desired one on her table. The punch glass stand illustrates a specimen of this type of ornamental useful table ware. (See illus. facing p. 90.)

The Russian Service made to the order of the Empress Catherine II of Russia, was the great central achievement to which all led up, and from which later successes emanated. It was to the accomplishment of this that Wedgwood directed every energy ; it was the greatest honour that could be paid to a manufacturer, and no stone was left unturned that would assist him in any way to satisfy so great a command.

The history of this service, the full description of its composition, the details of its decoration, and all other particulars referring to it, have been so ably and fully dealt with by Dr. Williamson in his book on *The Russian Service* that it is not necessary to repeat it here. We would refer the reader to that book and content ourselves with just this reference to the fact that it was the dominating cause for the demand that

[1] From the old " drawing book " (Etruria Museum).

arose from the British Isles and the Continent for Queensware, leading to its phenomenal and rapid development and the demand for it in all its various forms.

The tea table was equally well furnished : teapots, sugar boxes, cream jugs, caddies were made in quantities, in services of all sorts of compositions and in every one of the various patterns then in demand.

Leaving the table and looking at the more strictly ornamental use of the ware, we find a very great variety of vase forms, flowerpots and holders, for drawing-room, hall and boudoir.

Ware for these purposes was decorated in many ways by several processes. As Queensware proper it usually took the form of plain glaze or relief ornament upon the cream colour, sometimes in the same colour and occasionally in other coloured clays, often with very elaborately enriched knobs and handles. Of this type those shown facing p. 74 are examples.

The Cream Colour body was used also as a base upon which to use other coloured clays in the form of a decoration made with " slip " (liquid clay), and this was used in imitation of marble or agate or other natural bodies ; this slip was applied either by means of dipping the piece in the mixture or by pouring the mixture upon the piece and finishing afterwards. (See illus. facing p. 89.)

As these styles continued in favour for a number of years, a very great number of vases, flowerpots, bulb-pots, bowls and even tea ware, was made in them, the beauty of the marking and veining of the intermingling clays always forming the chief attraction of the piece, but this was at times accentuated and enhanced by the application of cream coloured relief ornament in swags of laurel leaves and berries or drapery, and the addition of ornate mask or scroll handles and knobs ; these embossed portions were generally further enriched by leaf gilding, unfired, which accounts in most cases for all traces of it having been removed by dusting and cleaning during the course of a hundred years or more.

Another decoration used for the same class of ornamental ware was obtained by dipping the cream colour vase in a coloured slip, and when stiffened sufficiently to handle, it was decorated by means of removing certain parts with a tool, showing the cream colour underneath. In this way also some very beautiful effects were produced upon the " engine turning " lathe and with the use of runners. (See illus. facing p. 89.)

The original Queensware illustrated catalogue sent out by Wedgwood has so many points of interest about it and the engravings are so beautifully executed that it is produced here in miniature. There are only nine plates showing thirty-five articles, and the original reason for its compilation reads :—

" It being impossible to send specimens . . . and
" the Names conveying but a very imperfect Idea of
" the Forms, it has been thought proper to send a few
" Prints of the Pieces, which will explain their Uses,
" and show their Forms better than could be done by
" Words alone." [1]

[1] From the original " Queensware " Catalogue, *circa* 1770–80.

This catalogue, of which the only existing copies are probably those in the Etruria Museum, is in itself an antique.

It has never been reproduced before, and has a legitimate place in this volume.

The catalogue from which these illustrations are taken is in French, and has a list of the hundreds of articles made " in complete Table and Dessert Services, " Tea and Coffee Setts, and other useful Articles, plain, " gilt, or embellished with Enamel Paintings in various " Manners." [1]

1. Pierced Fruit Basket.
2. Gravy Ladle.
3. Tureen.
4. Vegetable Dish.
5. Glacier.
6. Twin Salt Cellar and Tray.
7. Glass Stand.
8. Gravy Warmer.
9. Candlestick.
10. Sauce Boat and Stand.
11. Sauce Boat and Stand.
12. Sauce Boat and Stand.
13. Sauce Tureen and Stand with Ladle.
14. Candlestick.
15. Candlestick.
16. Monteith.
17. Oyster Plate or Hors d'œuvres Dish.
18. Soup Dish and Cover.
19. Egg Poacher.
20. Asparagus Pan.
21. Pierced Fruit Dish.
22. Oil Cruet.
23. Ice Cream Cup.
24. Tureen.
25. Salad Bowl.
26. Egg Cup.
27. Tureen.

---

[1] From the original " Queensware " Catalogue, *circa* 1770–80.

Pl. 1

PLATE I.

(*From the first Cream Colour Catalogue.*)

1. PIERCED FRUIT BASKET.
2. GRAVY LADLE.
3. TUREEN.

(Etruria Museum.)

[*To face page* 94.

PLATE 4.

(From the first Cream Colour Catalogue.)

10, 11 & 12. SAUCE BOATS.

13. SAUCE TUREEN WITH LADLE.

14. CANDLESTICK.

(Etruria Museum.)

[*To face Pl*

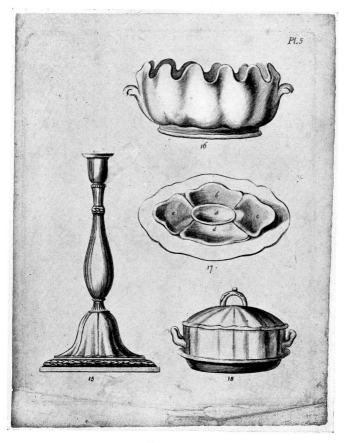

Pl.5

PLATE 5.

(From the first Cream Colour Catalogue.)

15. CANDLESTICK.
16. MONTEITH.
17. OYSTER PLATE OR HORS D'ŒUVRES DISH.
18. SOUP DISH AND COVER.

(Etruria Museum.)

[*To face Plate* 4.

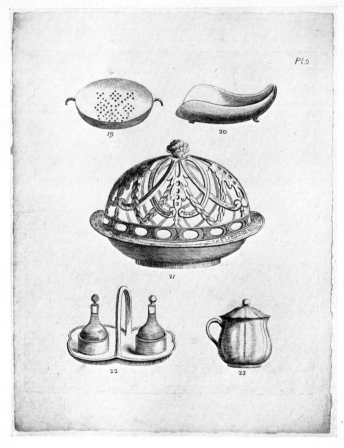

PLATE 6.

(*From the first Cream Colour Catalogue.*)

19. EGG POACHER.
20. ASPARAGUS PAN.
21. PIERCED FRUIT DISH.
22. OIL CRUET.
23. ICE CREAM CUP.

(Etruria Museum.)

[*To face page* 95.

28. Fruit Basket.
29. Stand for Same.
30. Sweetmeat Basket.
31. Sweetmeat Basket.
32. Pierced Chestnut or Orange Basket.
33. Salt Cellar.
34. Custard Cup.
35. Vegetable Dish.

Before leaving the vast area covered by the one branch of Etruria's manufacture classed under the title Queensware, it is proposed to pass over a long period during which the factory continued to produce with success the old patterns (so much so that it is necessary to exercise much judgment and care in selection to determine pieces which belong to the early period), and include some later styles of Wedgwood which have every right to be considered as part of a collection bearing this name, and as deceased artists' work is now allowed as " antique," the designs and craftsmanship of two at least of Etruria's great men are without apology given here, especially as their work is already being eagerly acquired whenever it appears in the sale room.

Emile Lessore made but a short stay in the Potteries —only five years—but that time was spent at Etruria with the exception of a few months on arrival. In a little pamphlet which he wrote, when forced to leave this country because of ill-health, in 1863, he expressed in glowing terms the comfortable conditions under which he was able and permitted to carry out freely any improvement that suggested itself to him in " colours of a stinted palette going through the fire," yet, as he goes on to say, " rich enough to produce tints adequate, not only to compete with oil colours, but far surpassing them in brilliancy."

He was a French painter who had worked independently all his life and because of cruel bereavement decided to leave his own country and seek a situation in another land as a diversion to grief. His last " hobby," as he puts it, was the Ceramic art, and naturally his steps were directed to Staffordshire.

Disregarding the fact that he had come to make a new ware, to depart from the beaten track, he meets the reproach which was then being made that Wedgwood had not changed for a century, with the remark : " Why ? When they are the leaders in a trade ; when " they have selected all the classical and pure prin- " ciples of fabrication ; when all the more beautiful " shapes of antiquity have been adopted by a manu- " factory, is it right to change these in order to meet " the modern taste ? God preserve them from such a " change ! It would be putting weeds where should be " laurels ! Is not Phidias always young after two " thousand years ? Who is the modern sculptor who " has replaced him ? "

In reply to French journals which reproached him for having quitted France and working exclusively for England, he said : " Painters ordinarily change their " national character before the works of the Masters, " their models. Thus, before Raffælle they are " Italians ; before Rubens, Flemish ; before Rem- " brandt, Dutch ; specially devoted to pottery, I have " become English at the Wedgwood's. There is my " answer."

His work was free in style, forcible in drawing and

PLATE 7.

(From the first Cream Colour Catalogue.)

 24. TUREEN.
 25. SALAD BOWL.
 26. EGG CUP.
 27. TUREEN.

(Etruria Museum.)

[*To face page* 96.

Pl. 8

PLATE 8.

(*From the first Cream Colour Catalogue.*)

28. FRUIT BASKET.
29. STAND FOR SAME.
30 & 31. SWEETMEAT BASKETS.

(Etruria Museum.)

[*To face Plate* 9.

PLATE 9.

(From the first Cream Colour Catalogue.)

32. PIERCED CHESTNUT OR ORANGE BASKET.
33. SALT CELLAR.
34. CUSTARD CUP.
35. VEGETABLE DISH.

(Etruria Museum.)

[*To face Plate* 8.

TWO VASES, QUEENSWARE, SNAKE HANDLES, PAINTED BY EMILE LESSORE.

(Wedgwood Institute, Burslem.)

colour, the designs were after the Boucher and Watteau style, and form a distinct island, as it were, which is separated from Etruria, but at the same time unmistakably wedded to it because of the form and technique of the ware upon which he painted.   (See illus. facing p. 97.)

Although he left England and returned to France in 1863, he continued to work for Wedgwood at his studio at Marlotte, Fontainebleau, until his death in 1875.   He signed his pieces in full.

L. Lessore

Thomas Allen, a native of the Potteries, was one of the finest ceramic figure painters.   He gained a scholarship in 1852 and was one of the first six students who formed the beginning of the Department of Practical Art founded by Prince Consort.   It was a practical result of the Great Exhibition of 1851, and the first head master was Mr. Henry Cole.   The students met then in the basement of Marlborough House, and afterwards the school became the Royal School of Art, South Kensington, now the Royal College of Art.

Allen painted some very beautiful figures, and heads, in a most finished style, and helped to form what was acknowledged during the mid-Victorian age as the correct type of painting for the nude and semi-draped figure upon China and porcelain.   He was also responsible for many of the dinner ware patterns, to which form of design he turned his attention when the demand for figure painting had ceased.

He worked at Etruria for thirty years, from 1875 until 1905, when he retired, and died ten years after, at the age of eighty-four years.

His figure painting on pottery is now being sought after, and when it appears in the sale room is realizing good prices.   He signed his work Tho⁵. Allen, with the Staffordshire knot and date sometimes added, or often only T.A. in monogram form.

IV

BASALTES
WARE

CHAPTER IV

BASALTES WARE

The refinement of black—Form—The desire to make vases
—The untiring search for material—The first fruits—
Black porcelain or basaltes—Failures—Progress made
—Encouragement of wealthy and noble clients—Faulty
pieces—The method used for restoring them—Caution
to the novice collector—The outcry for these new vases—
The Bedford vase—Shapes and the old shape book—
The beauty of the old pieces—Its durability—Remarks
from the old catalogue—Etruscan painting—Its redis-
covery and adaptation by Wedgwood—Disparaging
remarks made upon it—The first six vases made at
Etruria—Bentley's influence—Extract from one of the
early catalogues—List of distinguished patrons—The
" patina " on basaltes—The range of shapes produced—
Other pieces, not vases—The " Wine " and " Water "
ewers.

THERE has always been a dignity, sedateness, and
refinement about black, irrespective of the material to
which it may be applied ; it seems to have the quality
which demands simplicity both in form and decoration,
for a bad outline in black asserts itself more forcibly
than in any colour, and elaboration of ornament in it
has an irritating effect upon the eye, while purity in
outline and restraint in any applied design have exactly
the opposite effect upon the mind and vision, a feeling
of tranquillity, a desire to restfully absorb the beauty
t presents.

careful consideration to the evidences which exist of the earlier forms of Black or Egyptian Ware, but although he uses the name " Basaltes " in connection with them, there is no reason to believe that this name was ever applied to such ware, which was generally classed under the one term Black ware whether glazed or unglazed, and regardless as to its being only a surface black or solid colour throughout.   We still uphold our contention that the vitreous " Black Porcelaine " of Wedgwood which he named " Basaltes " was the first of that particular type, so sought after and imitated by his contemporaries.

Here is the proof that as far as the making of basaltes was concerned it was only in the experimental stage at the Burslem Works, and the " first fruits " appeared eleven months afterwards, before the completion and entry into the works at Etruria.

Further proof may be deduced from the sentence which follows the last extract given, in the same letter. " There are 3 other imperfect ones to show " you a little into the light of our imperfections in the " manufacturing of these delicate compositions." [1]

That disappointment and patience went hand in hand over this period was an experience that was expected, and borne with that special type of philosophy with which Providence has graciously endowed the potter—more especially the pioneer potter—but even the latter has at times to seek consolation from a kindred spirit, and we notice the barely concealed appeal in the closing remark : " Every Vase in the " last Kiln were spoil'd. & that only by such a degree

[1] Wedgwood letters to Bentley, August 30, 1768.

" of variation in the fire as scarcely affected our cream
" colour bisket at all." [1]

Before six months had elapsed considerable progress
and success must have been achieved, for in February
of the next year, when Wedgwood was in London for
a time looking after the business there and selling his
vases and ornamental pieces to distinguished clients
with much enthusiasm, he gives details of his experi-
ences with such as Lady Holland and the Duke of
Marlborough, and says : " I could sell 50 or £100 worth
" per day if I had them," at the same time sending an
urgent request to Bentley at the Brick House to exert
himself to get the Works at Etruria finished and in
the meantime to let all the hands that could be spared
be put to work on vases, for two reasons, " that they
" may be bringing up for Etruria, & the great demand
" here may not be baulked." " Some large Black
" Vases " he asks for, and this request is evidently
based upon the fact that his success had become more
or less absolute in the material which six months
before had given so much trouble and disappointment.

However, it is not to be supposed that faulty pieces
were non-existent, in all probability they were as
numerous (if not more so) than the perfect ones, for
that condition of manufacture has always been, and
ever will be, the lot of the pottery manufacturer.
Therefore we may be allowed here to correct a fairy-
tale which has been always associated with the master
potter of Etruria, no doubt originally applied by some
enthusiastic and devoted admirer, and which has
persisted more or less through all the records that have

[1] Wedgwood letters to Bentley, August 30, 1768.

since been published. It is not true to say, nor is it reasonable to suppose, that Wedgwood smashed every piece of ware that was not absolutely perfect, that he walked round the pottery with the aid of a stick which he used after his leg had been amputated (1768, the very period we are now considering) and with it demolished those articles which did not come up to the high standard of perfection which he himself had set out to reach, exclaiming as he did so : " This won't do for Josiah Wedgwood." Such æsthetic behaviour is not in accordance with human nature, much less is it possible in commercial economy, and Wedgwood by no means despised commercial success. If he had resorted to the practice suggested by this drastic measure, his business would have been bankrupt long before he had made any headway. No! the fact that faulty pieces occur (" seconds " as they are called in the trade) is the natural consequence produced by a hundred causes in the process of manufacture, and there is always a fair percentage of these " seconds " which are faulty in only a minor degree, not detrimental to the useful or ornamental value of the article. From an artistic standpoint there is often no blemish at all, and many a purchaser outside the factory would fail to discover it. How many of the most prized and unique pieces are there in collections to-day which can be called technically " perfect " ? If the method assigned to Wedgwood were to be applied among these, where would the collections be ?

That Wedgwood did make that remark once, upon a special occasion, is quite possible ; we may suppose that he had before him a piece of bad work produced by a dilatory or careless workman, and for purposes of example and the setting up of a standard to be followed, he made use of the expression and sacrificed the piece. It cannot, however, be assumed from this that it was his usual practice, but may be quite probable as an isolated instance.

The idea which has universally been accepted that no vases, in any way imperfect ever left Etruria, is erroneous. At this time, when the business was being built up, cash was a very necessary item and it was essential that everything for which a market could be found should be disposed of; therefore much ware of artistic and intrinsic value was saved and prepared for this purpose. It must be remembered that no " seconds " were made—they happened accidentally in the oven where the element " which no man can tame " had control—and it is fair to assume that only that which was worthy of preservation was allowed to pass the censorship of so keen an enthusiast as Wedgwood, whose integrity in business has always remained undisputed.

Perhaps a statement like this is now made for the first time, but facts must be faced, and reference to such a document as that from which the following is extracted gives without question the answer to those who would adhere to the romance of the " fairy-tale " quoted above :—

" I have settled a plan & method with Mr. Coward " (the famous wood carver who worked for the Brothers Adam, Architects of the Adelphi, London) " to tinker " all the black Vases that are crooked, we knock off

" the feet and fix wood ones, black'd, to them, those
" with tops, or snakes want^g are to be supply'^{d} in the
" same way.   I wish you could send me a parc^l of
" these Invalids by Sundays Waggon, as he wishes
" to have w^t we can furnish him wth of each sort
" together." [1]

Such success attended this genuine endeavour to
supply the demand for vases, and the satisfaction that
was given was evidently so appreciated, that a further
letter was written to Bentley just a month later, giving
some account of the progress made in reclaiming some
of these maimed works of art and transferring them
from the warehouse shelf to the mantelshelves and
cabinets of eager customers : " He has patched up
" some & bronzed others of the invalids, & sold them
" & serves the old creamcolour, & Gilt ones in the same
" way, & we have doctered, I won't say Tinkered, near
" £100 worth of what we deem'd reprobates here,
" & by next weeks end I believe shall not have a single
" waster left.   I have got an excellent cement, which
" we can even mould into ornaments, which grow
" nearly as hard as the ware & scarcely to be dis-
" tinguish'^{d} from it, with this we have done the Vases
" intended to be sold as seconds, & have converted
" them into best —   In short we are arriv'd to such
" a degree of perfection in the Art of V : making &
" V : mending that we have not had two seconds in
" the three last ovenfulls, nor even a single one that
" I know of." [2]

---

[1] Wedgwood's letter to Mrs. Wedgwood, February 23, 1769.
[2] Wedgwood letter to Bentley, March 23, 1769.

Each of these "invalids" had as much care and expense bestowed upon it as the "best" or perfect pieces, and the fact that a foot was crooked, or handle dropped or broken during firing, did not detract from the artistic value of the workmanship if such defect could be remedied; and if it was thought advisable and profitable for so competent a craftsman as Coward to accomplish the restoration, then surely we may assume that the ultimate result was worthy of those who undertook it, and the final possessor was satisfied with the bargain.

But a word of caution may be given here to the novice collector: "Go warily," for after such a new revelation, one imagines that there may be a sudden discovery of vases that were originally "restored" by Coward with wooden feet and handles, for Wedgwood & Bentley! Any such find would be extremely interesting, if genuine, and undoubtedly antique and valuable.

The author of these notes knows that such pieces do still exist, having been preserved in families that have possessed them since the time when they were first restored and sold and which have never passed into the market since. In such cases the "tinkering" or "doctering" has its own antiquity and added interest.

The outcry for vases came spontaneously from the very highest among his customers whose numbers increased rapidly among the nobility, and the inability to produce quickly enough caused incessant and untiring application. "I have got the Bassreliefs from "Mrs. Landres, have got some figures modeled for the

" tops & shoulders of Vases, some handles, pedestals,
" &c." [1]

It was at this time that the first reference to statu-
ettes is made, and is directly in connection with the
Basaltes " body " : " I am collecting some figures
" (Antique) to be made in Etruscan Earth, Mr. Cham-
" bers, & many others have a high opinion of them to
" mix with the Vases, by both these articles I hope we
" shall make a revolution in the chimneypieces, &
" strip them of their present Gaudy furniture of
" patch'd & painted figures." [2]

There was one vase which seems to have received
an unusual amount of admiration, and was called the
" Bedford Vase." Unfortunately this cannot be traced
with certainty now, but it was evidently one of the
first made that had a relief medallion. Much comment
was made upon it, and all in a congratulatory strain.
Wedgwood's reference to it shows how this was one
of the encouraging forces which led him to the class
of relief figure decoration which afterwards became so
completely connected with his name : " The Bassrelief
" upon the Medalion of the Bedford Vase is universaly
" admir'd wch I look upon as a propitious omen for
" that species of ornamenting, we have about a doz^{n}
" of them ord^{d}—all to be the very first that come.
" Mr. Cox has been running about with one (by desire)
" to several Noblemen this Even^{g} & says I must ord^{r}
" 1000, he says the Medallion alone wo^{d} sell it." [3]

In a volume of this kind that is admittedly only a
chat upon the productions of one factory, no exhaustive

[1] Letter from London, February 1769.   [2] *Ibid.*   [3] *Ibid.*

research can be attempted, so great is the mass of
manuscripts of all classes, letters, orders, notes, recipes,
ovenbooks, etc., etc., which have to be consulted and
tabulated ; but it must be at once conceded that
it is impossible to place with any accuracy the date
at which certain shapes made their appearance, except
in a few cases.   In vases alone there have been thousands of forms made at Etruria in many shapes, a series
which have ranged from 3 inches to 18 inches, but it
is correct to say, and may be a surprise to many to
know, that the number actually issued by Wedgwood
during his lifetime was only about 250.   The old
Shape Book shows that about 400 ornamental pieces
in all were made, and of these the true vases did not
number more than stated above, the remainder being
such decorative pieces as ewer vases, lamps, tripods
for use as candelabra, single candlesticks, flower-
holders with pierced grids, pedestals for vases, fancy
pots for growing bulbs in water, flowerpots, bowls,
baskets, inkstands, coffee, tea and chocolate pots,
with cups and saucers, butterdishes.   There is only
one game pie dish shown, the rather large variety of
this class of table ware followed chiefly during the
second period which started after the death of
Josiah I in 1795.   Only three large centrepieces are here
recorded, one being the two sphinxes supporting the
very ornate, quatrefoil, oval-shaped vase.   The wine
and water ewers belong to the early period and also
the Triton candlesticks.

Nearly all the first hundred shapes were vases made
for the decoration of chimney pieces and cabinets, and
were purely ornamental ; and being so, were produced in

the different wares which had so great a sale at that time, namely, " Cream Colour," " Agate," " Marbled," " Pebbled " and " Sprinkled," as well as in " Basaltes " and afterwards in " Jasper." They varied only slightly in shape but differed widely in applied decoration, more especially when the engine turning lathe was used for the enrichment of certain portions.

The original estimate of the beauty and value of this particular " Black Porcelaine " is worthy of close consideration, the more so at the present time when over one hundred and forty years have passed since it was first produced. Everything that was claimed for it has been abundantly realised during the intervening years : " A fine Black Porcelaine, having " nearly the same properties as the Basaltes ; resisting " the Attacks of Acids ; being a Touch-stone to " Copper, Silver and Gold; admitting of a good Polish, " and capable of bearing to be made red hot in a " Furnace, frequently, without Damage." [1]

The durability and vitreous nature of this material, and the way in which it retained the sharpness and detail of any modelling, tool mark or ornament, rendered it particularly suitable also for the preservation of any work of art, which in any other material, even metal, would have suffered from the variations of heat or damp, and this property was fitly described in the same catalogue from which the extract above is taken : " The black composition, having the Appear- " ance of antique Bronze, and so nearly agreeing in " Properties with the Basaltes of the Ægyptians, no

[1] A catalogue published in 1779.

" Substance can be better than this—it seems to us—
" to preserve as many fine Works of Antiquity and of
" the present Age as we can, in this composition ; for
" when All Pictures are faded and rotten, when Bronzes
" are rusted away, and all the excellent Works in
" Marble dissolved, then these Copies, like the antique
" Etruscan Vases, will probably remain, and transmit
" the Works of Genius, and the Portraits of illustrious
" Men, to the most distant Times. Those who duly
" consider the Influence of the fine Arts upon the
" human Mind, will not think it a small Benefit to the
" World to diffuse their Productions as widely, and to
" preserve them as long as possible : for it is evident,
" Multiplying Copies of the fine Works in durable
" Materials, must have the same Effect upon the Arts
" as the Invention of Printing has upon the Sciences ;
" by these Means the principal Productions of both
" kinds will be for ever preserved." [1]

The black ware was used as a foundation for a style
of encaustic painting in colours, mainly in red and
white, and in this which was termed " in the Etruscan
Style " in the old catalogue, a great variety of ware was
made—vases for decoration of chimney pieces and
mantels, flower-holders, and flowerpots for the table,
both for roots and the dressing with flowers, inkpots,
ecritoires, candelabra, tea ware, etc. These pieces are
generally characterised by a beautiful finish, both in
the surface, the lightness of the making, and the
delicacy of the painting upon them. The style was
directly suggested by the paintings on the Etruscan

[1] A catalogue published in 1779.

vases which were brought over to this country by Sir William Hamilton, and are now in the British Museum, although the method of painting was different. The *motifs* of design soon developed upon other lines and became quite an original departure in decoration, the solid black and naturally beautiful polish of the background lending itself admirably to the treatment. There are not a great many pieces left to us, but those that remain have a technique about them which convinces at once that the outcry and demand for them when they first appeared were warranted. The range was really a very great one, for the variety that was offered by the old catalogue shows how many ingenious changes were rung on the adaptations to different uses and on the different methods of treatment, either plain, slightly or fully decorated. A few extracts will show clearly the great number and variety of articles produced, and these will also form a useful guide or reference to the collector.

" Various kinds of Lamps and Candelabria, useful " and ornamental— These Lamps are both of the " variegated Pebble and black Composition. They " bear the Flame perfectly well, and are fit for Cham " bers, Halls, Stair-Cases, &c.

" The Tripod Lamps with several Lights are highly " enriched, and will be suitable Ornaments for the " finest Apartments.

" The Candlelabria are after antique Models—

" Ornamental Vases of antique Forms. These Vases " are adapted for the Ornament of Chimney Pieces, " Cabinets, Bookcases, &c. They are from six Inches

I.

2.   3.   4.

ENCAUSTIC PAINTING ON BASALTES.

1. KETTLE.

(Victoria and Albert Museum.)

2. CREAM JUG.   3. TEAPOT.   4. CUP AND SAUCER.

(Etruria Museum.)

[To face page 114.

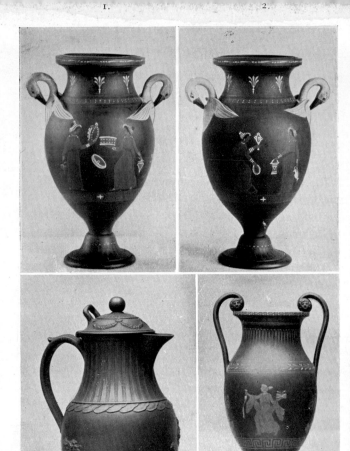

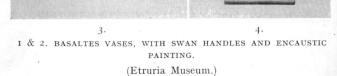

3.   4.

1 & 2. BASALTES VASES, WITH SWAN HANDLES AND ENCAUSTIC
PAINTING.

(Etruria Museum.)

3. BASALTES COFFEE JUG, RELIEF DECORATION, WITH HINGED
COVER.

4. BASALTES VASE, ENCAUSTIC PAINTING.

(Wedgwood Institute, Burslem.)

[To face page 115.

" to eighteen or twenty Inches high. They are
" generally sold in Pairs, or Sets of three, five, or seven
" Pieces." [1]

There is a great deal written in this old catalogue
about the painting on these vases, which are acknowledged copies " with the utmost exactness " from the
antique more especially to be found in the most choice
and comprehensive collection of Sir William Hamilton
" which to the Honour of the Collector, and of this
" Nation, and for the Advantage of our Artists, is now
" placed in the British Museum."

The art of painting in the manner of the Etruscans
was supposed to have been lost, and this was the
general opinion of all the connoisseurs and antiquaries
of the time, who gave such a description of the difficulties of the art as was sufficient to damp all hopes of
success. Fortunately Etruria had been working and
made considerable progress in a process of painting
with colours which differed entirely from the enamel
colours in general use. This process gave no glassy
lustre to the surface, and imitated exactly the paintings
on the Etruscan Vases, giving the advantages of light
and shade in various colours, and rendering the painting
durable without the effect of a varnished or glassy
surface.

This class of painting was also used for a series of
tablets suitable for inlaying into furniture, which were
made in sizes that could be introduced into mantel-
pieces or in such diminutive proportions that they
were mounted in bracelets and other articles of
jewellery.

[1] A catalogue published in 1779.

On these " Plates of artificial Basaltes," subjects, figures and others, were beautifully executed in a variety of colours with success—the colours did not run out of drawing ; they were smooth, durable, and without any vitreous glare, and were, and still are, acknowledged to be in the most refined taste.

So much attention was paid to these encaustic painted pieces, and so much invention, skill, time, and expense lavished upon them, that we have been tempted to dwell upon the subject.   There were many failures, few successes ; the difficulty of producing perfect specimens gave them a value in proportion to the time expended upon their production. For several reasons this section of Etruria's efforts has received only partial notice, probably because they were very faithful copies of the antique, which soon after ceased to be in favour, or because their general appearance was considered sombre and funereal, or again, because to-day the chance of finding specimens is more remote, but from the ceramic connoisseur's standpoint there is no ware which calls forth the admiration of technique more completely than this, and it is a section which will amply repay any who are enticed into the study of it.

Various remarks have been made upon the general effect of the painting upon these vases from an artistic point of view, and some are disparagingly made, such as " the imitation is vastly inferior," referring to the copy of a subject in Sir Wm. Hamilton's book and, " he aimed at mechanical rather than artistic perfec- " tion.   The touch of such enamel painters as he could " procure for the drawing of his figures is generally tame

1.   2.

I & 2. PAIR OF TRITON VASES, BASALTES, RELIEF DECORATION.

3.   4.   5.

3 & 5. PAIR OF EWER VASES, BASALTES, RELIEF DECORATION.

(Wedgwood Institute, Burslem.)

4. LAMP, TWO BURNERS, BASALTES.

(British Museum.)

[To face page 116

1.

2.

1. LAMP, TRIANGULAR FOOT, BASALTES.
2. VASE, ENGINE-TURNED AND RELIEF DECORATION, BASALTES.

(Wedgwood Institute, Burslem.)

3.

3. LAMP, TRIPOD FOOT, BASALTES.

(Etruria Museum.)

[To face page 117.

"and spiritless and their timid pencilling is in the "greatest contrast to the freedom and dexterity of the "work they were striving to imitate." Now this appears to us scarcely a fair estimate ; it must be remembered that at that time no artists existed in the Potteries, and it was not a matter of procuring any painters that could be found, but producing them from any promising material that was at hand sufficiently capable of training and instruction. It must have been uphill work, and every credit should be given to Wedgwood for the result which he was able to obtain which was passed by the keenly critical connoisseurs of his day, and as far as we are concerned the pieces that remain to our day compare very favourably with the originals, and in many technical qualities far exceed them.

The six vases "thrown" by Wedgwood while Bentley turned the wheel, on the opening day of the Etruria Works—June 13, 1769—were Basaltes, afterwards decorated with encaustic painting. The latter was done, as was much more of this work, at the decorating works which were under the direct supervision of Bentley in Chelsea. After the finishing and handling of these vases was complete they were fired and sent to London and are referred to in a letter from Wedgwood to Bentley five months later. " The six " Etruscan Vases, three handled sent to you a fortnight " since were those we threw & turn'd the first at " Etruria, & sho'd be finish'd as high as you please, " but not sold they being first fruits of Etruria." [1]

The perfecting of the encaustic painted ware was for the time the ruling passion of Wedgwood and the

[1] Wedgwood to Bentley, November 19, 1769.

partner Bentley ; both were equally enthusiastic about it, and the latter was undoubtedly a man of exceptional refinement of taste. This would in all probability be conclusively settled were it not that the much-prized letters from Bentley to Wedgwood have unfortunately been lost. It was the first direct result of the partnership in the " Ornamental Works " showing the immense value of Bentley's knowledge of antique art when applied to direct and inspire Wedgwood's wonderful technical ability.

The key-note is unmistakably sounded in the estimate of their efforts given in their own catalogue, from which we extract the last reference we have space to make upon this section of the basaltes :—

" A Competitition for Cheapness, and not for Excel-
" lence of Workmanship, is the most frequent and
" certain Cause of the rapid Decay and entire Destruc-
" tion of Arts and Manufactures.

" An ordinary Piece of Goods, for common Use, is
" always dearer than the best of the kind, yet an ordi-
" nary and tasteless Piece of Ornament is not only dear
" at any Price, but absolutely useless and ridiculous.

" There is a mistake those who are not acquainted
" with the particular Difficulties of an Art, are apt to
" fall into.

" They frequently observe that a handsome Thing
" may be as cheap as an ugly one.—Even suppose an
" Artist has the true Idea of the kind of Beauty at
" which he aims, how many lame and unsuccessful
" Efforts does he make in his Design, and every Part
" of it, before he can please himself ? And suppose

" one Piece is well composed and tolerably finished ;
" as in Vases and encaustic Paintings, for instance,
" where every succeeding Vase and every Picture, is
" made, not in a Mould or by a Stamp, but separately,
" by the Hand, with the same Attention and Diligence
" as the first how difficult must it be to preserve the
" Beauty of the first Model. Beautiful Forms and
" Compositions are not to be made by Chance ; and
" they never were made, nor can be made in any kind
" at a small Expence : but the Proprietors of this
" Manufactory have the satisfaction of knowing, that
" they do not manufacture for those who estimate
" Works of Ornament by their Magnitude, and who
" would buy Pictures at so much a Foot : they have
" been happy in the Encouragement and Support of
" many illustrious Persons, who judge of the Works of
" Art by better Principles ; and so long as they have
" the Honour of being thus patronized, they will
" endeavour to support and improve the Quality and
" Taste of their Manufactures." [1]

A list of patrons who possess " Specimens of these
kinds of Vases " is included and is headed by " Our
Illustrious Sovereigns "—that is, George III and Queen
Charlotte—and is followed by the Empress of Russia
(Catherine II), the Kings of Poland, Prussia, Sweden,
Denmark, and Portugal, and twenty other names of
Grand Dukes, Electors, Princes, Dukes, Marquises,
Barons, Landgraves, etc., showing what a hold these
painted Etruscan Vases had already obtained.

The basrelief vases in black have always proved

[1] A catalogue published in 1779.

themselves worthy of the collector's attention, the material itself is of such a beautiful texture, and with constant handling and dusting takes a delightful " patina " that is not excelled by that which we associate with bronze. As has been remarked before, the sharpness of detail is not lost in the firing, it simply contracts and seems to become more pronounced the harder and more vitreous the body becomes.

The range of shapes in these basaltes vases is just as complete as the shape book itself, for everything that was made in the other wares was also made in this black, but this clay had the advantage of being more plastic and workable than some of the other clays, and so there is in reality a greater range than is found in any other section—even the Jasper itself—for some large pieces which were impossible in Jasper were successfully made in basaltes, and as the reliefs were made in the same clay as the body of the vase, they had an absolute affinity, the want of which was a very real cause of disaster in the case of the white reliefs upon the coloured ground.

While practically all the shapes and designs found in Jasper have their replicas in basaltes, there were many large vases made in basaltes which were never attempted in Jasper and these were indeed noble pieces which measured from 20 inches to 36 inches in height, sometimes plain, and at others decorated with relief borders or friezes of figures. There could not have been a very great number of these made, because of the extra and unusual arrangements that were necessary for their manufacture, the special appliances wanted for their manipulation, and the accommodation of them in the

1.   2.   3.

1 & 3. VASES, BASALTES, RELIEF DECORATION; SUBJECT OF FRIEZE,
"THE MUSES."

2. VASE, BASALTES, RELIEF DECORATION; SUBJECT OF FRIEZE,
"PRIAM BEGGING THE BODY OF HECTOR."

4.   5.   6.

4. BUST, BASALTES, "HOMER."
5. INKSTAND, BASALTES, EGYPTIAN DESIGN.
6. BUST, BASALTES, ON PEDESTAL, "ARIADNE."

(Wedgwood Institute, Burslem.)

[To face page 120.

1.   2.

3.   4.

LARGE CIRCULAR PLACQUES.

1 & 2. BLACK BASALTES; SUBJECT, "HERCULANEUM FIGURES."
3. CREAM COLOUR; SUBJECT, "CENTAUR."
4. CREAM COLOUR; SUBJECT, "POLYPHEMUS."

(Victoria and Albert Museum.)

[*To face page* 121.

oven. We can easily imagine that their production was not in the ordinary routine but always unusual. They may be regarded as almost unique specimens and are to-day quite scarce.

There are ornamental pieces which can scarcely be called vases, which form a separate section and which have always been made in basaltes (such as centre-pieces, tripods, and lamps), including also the wine and water ewers assigned to Flaxman ; but although these latter are almost invariably basaltes, some were made at first in Jasper with varying success, but very few of them exist to-day.[1] These ewers make a fine pair in black, and in this material fewer technical difficulties presented themselves, so that it became the recognised form in which great numbers have been made and are still produced ; but considerable care and discrimination is required when judging. Periods of decadence have occurred, due in every case to the commercial clamour for a cheaper article, which necessitates the rushing and scamping of work, not allowing the workman sufficient time to put into his work that knowledge and technique which he possesses. Still, there have been times when keen and serious attention to standard and the realisation of technical perfection have rewarded the craftsman of Etruria. The artisan to-day has the ability, and with the accumulation of the dexterity and invention of succeeding generations can produce work which will vie with that of his ancestors.

[1] A pair are in the Bury Art Gallery, a pair in the Nottingham Castle collection (blue and white), and a pair in the Haworth collection (blue and white). One other is known in sage and white.

The Placques, Tablets, Medallions, Cameos, and Intaglios, which were made in such a variety, in this basaltes body, will be dealt with in the chapter reserved to that section, and also the Figures and Busts which collectively form so striking an example of achievement in portraiture as well as in ceramic skill.

V

JASPER
WARE

CHAPTER V

JASPER WARE

In the whole realm of pottery there is to those who
have any knowledge of the difficulties involved no
word that fires the enthusiast or inspires reverence
in the practical potter like that which is the title of
this chapter. It suggests a sense of super-refinement
to the art connoisseur, a perfect mastery over the most
refractory material to the manufacturer, and an
almost magical control over that fickle element, fire,
to the chemist.

Several emulated Wedgwood's efforts in this direction ; some travelled with great success along original

lines, others were content to follow Wedgwood closely, while the greater number were mere copyists inevitably doomed to final oblivion. After all that has been said, it remains an outstanding fact that to Wedgwood must be given the whole credit for the invention and introduction of this particular porcelain body and its application to the special uses to which he put it, no one since has improved it, nor has anyone evolved a new way in which its beautiful qualities can be so completely displayed.

What is the history of Jasper ? To trace it fully would be a stupendous task, but it will be sufficient to give an idea of the years of patient research, experiment, and failure which eventually led up to the final perfecting of this material which was to have such an influence upon the productions of our premier potter, as well as upon the whole industry.

When we look at the hundreds of " trial " pieces, for this " body " which he left behind in his marvellous collection, we are amazed at the variety they present. They may be almost compared to that which one sees when gazing at the pebble beach ; every shade of white, yellow, blue, grey, green, brown, and black seems to confront us. This alone would be sufficient to account for a whole life's work, yet it was only one portion of his, and though important, it does not really stand out conspicuously from other series of experiments which he carried out as completely and in as great a numerical range.

The first mention of the " white body " is in July 1774, when he writes almost despairingly to the effect that he has no knowledge nor can any be acquired

VASE, JASPER; SUBJECT, "APOTHEOSIS OF HOMER."
(*This is the one referred to in Wedgwood's letter, see page* 141.)
(British Museum.)

[*To face page* 126.

PAIR OF VASES FOR BULB GROWING, JASPER.

but from experience, for he was using materials not known or tried before, and therefore cannot promise success when dealing with large masses, nor has he raw materials to experiment with :—

" M— Stone, & Spath fusible are the two articles I
" want, & several samples I have of the latter are so
" different in their properties that no dependence can
" be had upon them. They have plagued me sadly
" of late." [1]

Trials proved that one lump would fire a fine white and the next vary so much as to be a cinnamon colour ; one would be melted to a glass, while the next would be as dry as a tobacco pipe. The importance of mastering this difficulty pressed so greatly upon him that a week later we find in a further letter the remark : " I must go into Derbyshire myself in search of the Spaith fusible." [2] But in the meantime Hope had lent her influence, and the next message is a cheery one : " I believe I shall make an excellent white body, " and with absolute certainty, without the fusible " Sparr." [3] Progress was evidently made in this new " white body " during the latter part of 1774, for in December he writes : " From several late series of " experiments I have no reason to doubt being able to " give a fine white composition any tint of fine blue " ; [4] and he mentions the making of many more experiments which cause him to be so busy that this

[1] Wedgwood to Bentley, July 21, 1774.
[2] *Ibid.*, July 30, 1774.
[3] *Ibid.*, September 3, 1774.
[4] *Ibid.*, December 18, 1774.

short account of success is all that he has time to send, with some few results in the shape of some " seals " and the remark, " these first seedlings which I have no " doubt will in time become most beautifull Plants."

The difficulties of 1774 in this respect seem to have been overcome, the successful result of all his efforts is clearly announced, and is a strongly joyous feature of his letter on January 1, 1775, where, first commenting on a note in Bentley's letter to him, he says he is " glad to think that the ' white body ' is of sufficient " fineness—and has no reason to doubt of being able " to continue it so," and adds : " The blue body I am " likewise absolute in of almost any shade, & have " likewise a beautifull Sea Green, and several other " colors, for grounds to Cameos, Intaglios, &c., & " shall be able to make almost any of our Cameos " in figures from the Herculaneum size to the least " Marriage of Cupid &c, & in heads from Peter the " great to the smallest Gem for Rings, of the blue, " & other color'd grounds, with the Figures & Heads " in our fine white composition." [1]

The actual date, therefore, of the birth of the Jasper " body " may be given as 1775, but although the mixings and materials were settled and proved, the actual adaptation of it to the various articles which were subsequently made had not yet begun ; in fact, at the first it is only mentioned in connection with small pieces, such as cameos and seals, and the difficulties of making and firing vases and tablets had yet to come.   These difficulties were ever present, necessi-

[1] Wedgwood to Bentley, January 1, 1775.

tating the strictest and most careful supervision, the details of which occupy a very large part of his correspondence.

The introduction and perfecting of the Jasper Ware must be considered as a sort of sacred charge which Wedgwood imposed upon himself ; it was a " hobby," but it was more than that, for the earnest and pains-taking endeavour which he constantly bestowed upon it, and the untiring efforts made throughout his life to make it what it actually afterwards became—a triumph of ceramic skill—could never have made it a profitable undertaking. He seemed to take no heed of expense : the one aim was perfection. To reach this he was lavish in the acquisition of any material that would aid him, either in the purchase of designs and models, or the engaging of suitable artists, sculptors or workmen, and in doing this he collected a mass of " copy " which never was used, and which remains to-day. It must be remembered that at the period when the Jasper came into being he had already been commercially successful far beyond his expectations, and his works were hard put to it to supply the orders which poured in ; his continual cry was for more hands to cope with this or that demand.

This regular flow was " grist to the mill," and he was thus given the opportunity to indulge his ardent desire and consuming passion, that of giving to his artistic and aristocratic clientele (who encouraged him with their enthusiastic appreciation and pur-chasing power) this child of his brain, his beloved Jasper. It was with him as it has always been with pioneers in Arts of Painting, Sculpture, Literature,

Science or Discovery, that profit has been reserved for those who follow. Looking at his vases in this light, the connoisseur has a possession which must not be reckoned in mere monetary value ; he has in each piece some of the individuality of the man himself, for every detail of this particular branch seems to have been made a personal matter, an impression confirmed by acquaintance with his letters, notes, receipt books, and other manuscripts and material.

The earliest record of the use of the name "Jasper" as given to this " body " seems to be in April 1775, when it is used in connection with the consignment of some goods to London : " We send some Jasper Candelsticks, " Inkstands, and other articles immediately wanted " to-day." [1]   This indicates that after achieving success with cameos and seals, it was not long before the making of pieces thrown on the wheel and turned upon the lathe had proved successful.   Here again is the evidence of " first fruits " as far as adaptability of the " body " to this type of manipulation was concerned.

Jasper vases were not made during the partnership of Wedgwood & Bentley—at any rate for sale purposes—they were evidently in the " offing " and had materialised as far as successful trial pieces, but it is a significant fact that no Jasper vase has been found with the stamp Wedgwood & Bentley upon it ; little square white plinths, having the mark, were made for the marbled and other vases, but if they are found attached to any Jasper vase they are not in their original position.

[1] April 1, 1775.

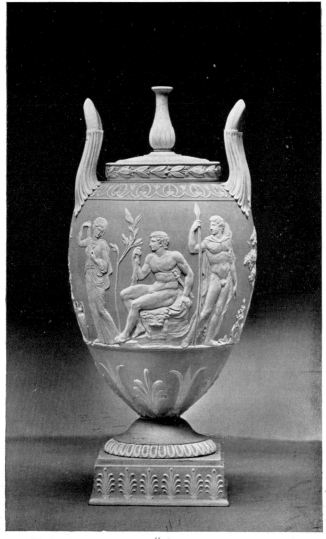

VASE, JASPER; SUBJECT, "HERCULES IN THE GARDEN
OF THE HESPERIDES."

(Wedgwood Institute, Burslem).

[*To face page* 130.

1.   2.

1. VASE, JASPER ; SUBJECT, " GRACES WATERING PEGASUS."
2. VASE, JASPER ; SUBJECT, " FRIEZE OF CUPIDS."

3.   4.   5.

3. CUSTARD CUP.
4. BOWL.   } *Part of a service.*
5. UNHANDLED CUP.

(Etruria Museum.)

[*To face page* 131.

The "Candelsticks" referred to above would probably be small taper holders for sealing purposes, and might have been made in either the white body or a pale blue or grey blue one; the inkstands and other articles were undoubtedly in other wares which had been inquired for.

The keen longing for Jasper vases, however, very soon asserts itself, and can never have been out of mind. It is referred to in the form of a query: "What "do you think of Vases of our fine blue body, with white "Laurel festoons, Medallions, &c?" And this vision of the possibilities of his new body is an alluring one, for his continued trials give him every encouragement and fire his ambition to greater efforts which alternate between success and failure for the three following years, and give occasion for much comment in his letters to his great friend and partner. Just one year after the first rejoicing over the successful conquest of the materials and mixings he says, with a certain amount of cautious reserve: "I believe I can now "assure you of a conquest, & a very important one "to us. No less than the firing of our fine Jasper & "Onyx with as much certainty as our Basaltes or "Black Ware. We had about 8 doz. of heads all "fired this new way, which I had tried a few times "before with so much success that I ventur'd to put "to above qu^{ty} to the test all at one firing, & they "were every one good, except a few accidents in "cracking, & scarcely any of them, but in respect to "firing they were perfect, & the two bodies, blue & "white agree perfectly together, &, as I manage "them now, it cannot be otherwise. So I am fully

" perswaded this new Art, which I have more & more
" reason to believe will be a very capital one to us,
" is completed, & brought to perfection, & I heartily
" give you joy of this last discovery which has given
" the finishing stroke to the Art." [1]

The works are busy on some larger basreliefs for
chimney pieces, etc.—" all with blue grounds "—
and these are to be sent to London in time for the
spring season, so that no time is found to enter into
improvements in useful ware : " for such a white ware
" as you mention, I must beg a longer time.   My hands,
" & my Head too have been too full of the business
" immediately before me—especially the completion
" of the Art of Jasper making which I was determin'd
" to conquer or give up before I enter'd seriously into
" any other capital improvement." [2]

Four days later we read : " As I have now com-
" pleted my Jasper, I shall now bend my attention
" to a white ware of some kind." [3]   All this shows what
an insatiable thirst he had for experimental research,
he never seemed to rest from it, and one success
was only an incentive to further exertion. This,
of course, accounts for the amount of work he got
through, and being, as his carefully tabulated trials
show, a most methodical man, he was always able
when he laid a thing down to take it up again exactly
at the point where he left it, though not without some
personal sacrifice and inconvenience. " I have not been
" on Horse back of a Month or I do not know how

[1] Wedgwood to Bentley, January 14, 1776.
[2] *Ibid.*   [3] *Ibid.*, January 18, 1776.

" long, but feel I want it very much. My Cabinet,
" & Experiment Books are the better for my confine-
" ment ; for having put the former into a little better
" order, & made Indexes to the latter, my knowledge
" lies straighter in my head, & I am considerably
" more learned than I was before I begun upon this
" good work." [1]

Through the early part of 1776 each oven produced
more successes, which must have been cheering to
both partners. There are many allusions in the
letters, as when Wedgwood writes to say that he had
" drawn more fine Jasper yesterday & not a single
" piece discolor'd, blister'd, or shewing any tendency
" to either of those disorders, so that I may now surely
" be confident of our being absolute in respect to
" firing this delicate substance." [2] But in spite of
all this enthusiasm and confidence in what his trials
and experience had taught him, he continually received
rebuffs which would have quenched the ardour of many
a one with less energy than he possessed, for at the
moment when the " firing " difficulties were overcome,
there came a return of the " composition " mysteries,
and he has to revert to these with the guarded remark,
" I have nearly managed my whimsical Jasper Composition."

Still, these throwbacks do not interfere seriously
with the onward movement, and confidence is shown
in the reference to the boast of a neighbouring manufacturer who had given out that he also had discovered
Jasper. " The boast of my Neighbour, that he had

[1] Wedgwood to Bentley, February 6, 1776.
[2] *Ibid.*, February 3, 1776.

9

" found it out is idle—I would as soon believe he had
" discover'd the Philosophers Stone — Besides — If I
" was to give him the rec^t, it would half ruin him, &
" quite tire him out before he could make anything
" of it—but the R-Ant^o [1] is made at the first essay.
" Everybody can make that color, & composition,
" but nobody, besides W & B can make Jasper." [2]

Another difficulty crops up in what has since been
termed " bleeding." That Wedgwood had this to
contend with very early is clearly shown : " In some
" things the blue shade which our ground is so apt
" to cast through the thin parts of the white, may be
" of advantage to the subject, as in the Armour by the
" side of the conquer'd Province — Any parts of
" Drapery which requires to be thrown back, or other
" apendages to the Figures — But when the naked
" part of the Figure is penetrated with the color of the
" ground, it is generally injurious — See the poor
" Queen's Nose, & many other Cameo's." [3] It has
often been stated that this " bleeding " is entirely
a modern feature due to an inability of the later
" Etruscans " to deal with the manufacture successfully, and that you will never find it in the old pieces.
That it did exist, however, is proved, and very beautifully finished pieces there are that possess it : " The
" risque is the same with one color as another, only
" in respect to staining the white a middle tint for
" the ground will stain the white less than a full
" color'd ground. But you told me in a former letter

[1] Red Body (Rosso Antico).
[2] Wedgwood to Bentley, July 5, 1776.
[3] *Ibid.*, July 9, 1776.

" that nobody bought a pale blue ground if a full
" color'd one lay near it, which induc'd me to attempt
" a deeper color, & the white has suffered by it." [1]

It is quite evident that the Jasper cameos, medallions and smaller tablets, which were at this time
being sent to London, were much appreciated, and
the many requests for other things in this beautiful
composition call forth the reply : " The Jaspers
" you want are put in hand, Viz, the Figure of Day
" & the 2 Baccanalian Figures, & though this said
" Jasper is extremely delicate, & difficult to manage,
" yet I hope to over come every difficulty — At least
" I mean to continue my attempts so long as I live
" a Potter. But in the interim I will make you Bass-
" reliefs of Red, Red & Black, or any other color in
" my power. If you think it will be prudent." [2]

Clearly, then, a return of trouble necessitated a
partial suspension of production and a further season
of application to overcome and master the defects,
and this appears to have been tackled with the usual
promptitude and attention, for barely a month afterwards more " good news " is sent : " I can tell you,
" we have had but one piece of Jasper crack'd of
" 5 or 6 Burnings, & I have reason to believe we have
" nearly conquer'd that difficulty, &, with small
" things, at least, shall proceed very currently. The
" Tablets I do not despair of, but that must be a
" work of time." [3]

All through this year he was continuing his trials
and adopting every possible device that he could to

[1] Wedgwood to Bentley, July 10, 1776.
[2] *Ibid.*   [3] *Ibid.*, August 8, 1776.

arrive at a stable article, sending the results of all his experiments to Bentley, whose advice, knowledge, and approval he sought at every turn. At times he must have been very disconsolate, and needed the encouragement which he undoubtedly received, but his spirit never flagged, and the determination to conquer was the compelling impulse which carried him forward. " I have sent a Jasper Tablet, short fired, " that you may see what state we are in ; we " have done with the cracking which teized us so " much in the former compositions and only want a " proper fire to make us absolute. When I tell you " that the fire this Tablet has gone through would " be sufficient for the Statues, & too hot for the small " ring Cameos, You will perceive some of the diffi- " culties we labor under in having a proper fire for " this delicate composition. However I shall perse- " vere, & hope, as all projectors do you know to " Conquer." [1]

Thus the pendulum would swing to and fro—a new body would come to grief in the existing method of firing ; when the firing was altered some difficulty with the body would appear. These unforeseen and continual happenings gave opportunities for unparalleled patience and perseverance which in the end was rewarded, but the care and vigilance exercised at the beginning could not be, and never was, relaxed. Such is the history of " potting."

This determination to make vases of Jasper was all-absorbing with both partners ; it was never abandoned, and indeed prompted all the experiments with the

[1] Wedgwood to Bentley, September 28, 1776.

various Jasper mixings of materials—but the goal
was far off and the most untiring efforts seemed for a
long time to result in little but failure.

The persistence with which this elusive problem was
attacked again and again is best shown in Wedgwood's
own words, which occur repeatedly in his letters with
surprisingly slight variation in phraseology, tending
to emphasise, after all, the monotonous regularity
of failure that fully explains the remark which was
applied to the boastful neighbour, who professed to
have arrived so easily at the point which cost Wedgwood such a struggle to reach : " Black blue grounds
" are what I have been attempting a long time, &
" have sometimes succeeded but much oftner mis-
" carried ; though both good, & the bad have been
" of the same mixture oweing to some differences in
" the fire which I cannot yet ascertain, or command.
" I shall pursue the object, as far as Cameos & Intag-
" lios, for Rings, but to reconcile our Black Body, in
" Vases, to admit of an union with the Jasper Body
" in Bassrelief Figures of pale blue, is an arduous
" attempt, to say the least of it. I can only observe
" upon this subject that there is no saying what may,
" or may not be done : not even after all the attempts
" we have made may have failed." [1]

Here is the true pioneer, and it is because of the
liberty permissible in a " chat " that one is prompted
to dwell upon it. When we look upon the much-prized
possessions in the hands of collectors of this particular
Jasper, notice the exquisite detail and finish of the
work, and the technical skill displayed, and consider

[1] Wedgwood to Bentley, September 30, 1776.

by what an uphill path, strewn with obstacles the height has been reached, we feel that the value of these vases cannot be overrated, and the more we are acquainted with the history of their birth and development the more surely will be our appreciation of their merits.

The exact period when Jasper vases came into being cannot be definitely located.   That all the patient work brought forth abundant results we know, and that the first essays were probably unimportant pieces, small hand lamps and taper candlesticks and such-like which led up to the making of the vase proper when the " body " had been sufficiently tested.   The shapes made were those included in the first four hundred as recorded in the old shape book referred to in the chapter on Cream Coloured Ware.   Wherever a shape number is known and the colour of body and general finish of the piece accord, the identification is, of course, simplified.   It must be borne in mind that all these old shapes and designs have been reproduced at later dates by the firm from the old records, moulds and designs, in materials approximating as nearly to the original as nature has been able to supply, and the old traditions and handicraft have been preserved by the descendants of both masters and workmen, so that the stamp impressed, WEDGWOOD, though a guarantee of genuineness, is no guide to age or period, and there are a score of other " marks " which have to come into consideration before a correct opinion can be given.   Experience and knowledge only can be of guidance here.   Certain it is that a great deal of very beautiful Jasper, more especially in the form of

1.   2.

I & 2. VASE, JASPER, STRAP WORK AND RELIEF DECORATION,
SHOWING REVERSIBLE COVER FOR USE AS A TAPER HOLDER.

3.

3 CUP AND SAUCER, JASPER, ENGINE-TURNED AND
RELIEF DECORATION.

(Etruria Museum.)

[To face page 138.

1. FLOWER HOLDER, JASPER, IMITATION OF RUIN.
2. FLOWER HOLDER, JASPER, IMITATION OF RUIN.

3 & 5. A PAIR OF SALT CELLARS, JASPER; SUBJECT,
FLAXMAN'S " DANCING HOURS."
4. CANDLESTICK, JASPER, RELIEF DECORATION AND
ENGINE-TURNING.
(British Museum.)

[To face page 139.

vases, was made during the period of the second Josiah, who was a most worthy follower of his illustrious father, and who multiplied and increased very largely the list of Jasper vases. He was a most able potter, and benefited to the full by the wonderful legacy which he inherited and which he worthily made use of. Too little has been said of his part in the work of Etruria, nor has he been credited with that which undoubtedly belongs to him, and this we say without detracting one iota of fame from him to whom the ceramic world owes so much. The son certainly profited from all the work of his predecessor, but it is only fair to say that he introduced much that was new and original, and perhaps more conspicuously so in the range of vases which were produced in Jasper during his régime. This is said because so many of our collections, public and private, have vases which are assigned to the first Josiah, and which in reality were never conceived either in shape or design until many years after his death. \

Unfortunately it is impossible in a work of this size to give a list even of the first four hundred shapes, and this would be of no use without illustrations; those seriously wanting information can obtain it from the source already mentioned, the Etruria Museum.

No book dealing with Wedgwood Ware would be complete without some mention of the Portland Vase—that masterpiece of potting which has commanded the reverence of all those who have made excursions into the mysterious and illusive " domain of body-mixing " and the prohibitive province of the oven, whose masterful element successfully bars all entrance, and whose dictates must be obeyed.

Mystery enshrines the birth and history of the original vase ; the highest intellects have formed conjecture and have romanced about it. Wedgwood's copy of it, which occupied his closest attention for about four years, has its own mystery and romance. A great deal has been written which will have to be unwritten, and proved facts will have to take the place of fiction, but the time is not ripe for full disclosures. It is sufficient now to say that there is no foundation whatever for the generally accepted idea that the original edition consisted of fifty copies which were subscribed for. So many copies never existed ; in fact, it is doubtful if a dozen left the works at Etruria during Wedgwood's lifetime.

The Etruria Works have at intervals made copies of this vase, using the original figure moulds and putting all detail and finish that the technical skill of the craftsman employed could command. An edition, for instance, was produced in 1878, but as these were all carefully undercut and polished by the lapidary, they may be distinguished the more readily by the latter's private mark upon them. But, after all, the total number is very limited, and the chance of a new aspirant acquiring an original is very remote.

The real history of Wedgwood's copy of the Portland Vase has yet to be written, and must be deferred to the time when data are complete.

One important vase which commands attention was the Homeric Vase,[1] and was considered by Wedgwood

[1] See illus. facing p. 126.

SQUARE PEDESTAL, JASPER, ADAPTED FOR BULB GROWING.
(Etruria Museum.)

BOWL, JASPER, "ARABESQUE" DESIGN.
(British Museum.)

[To face page 140.

I.   2.

1 & 2. PAIR OF VASES, JASPER, "SACRIFICE" FIGURES.

3.

3. BASKET AND STAND, JASPER, WITH BLUE, WHITE AND
GREEN STRAP WORK.

(Wedgwood Institute, Burslem.)

[*To face page* 141.

himself to be a *chef d'œuvre*. It is indeed a noble
piece in outline, proportion and detail, and has been
made in both Jasper and Basaltes. In Jasper it has
generally been made in pale blue and white, grey blue
and white, or black and white.

The principal subject is the " Apotheosis of Homer,"
and represents the deification of this greatest ancient
poet. Above are two attendant celestial beings, while
a female with a sceptre (emblematic of Royalty), and
a male (emblematic of learning and education), ador-
ingly witness the translation to the higher sphere.

The basrelief is one of the most graceful pieces of
Flaxman's modelling, who executed it in or about
1776, when only twenty-one years of age. There is
a distinctness in the grouping of the figures, and a
peculiarity in the folds and flow of the drapery, which
belong essentially to his style.

This vase is now in the British Museum, where it
has been since the time of its production, and cannot
be better described than in Wedgwood's own words
in a letter which he wrote to Sir William Hamilton
as a sort of postscript to a long series of questions and
requests for advice as to how he should most ade-
quately deal with the " Portland Vase " which had
so generously been lent to him by His Grace the Duke
of Portland to copy. He writes : " One word farther,
" & I have done. I have just now executed an order,
" by the direction of a merchant in Manchester, for
" an assortment of my jasper ornaments, with blue
" grounds & white figures,[1] which he tells me are
" for the King of Naples. If so, you will perhaps see

---

[1] These were vases or cabinet pieces, not placques.

" them in a short time,[1] and I mention this to beg
" the favour of your correction if you think any of
" them worth so much of your notice. One thing I
" persuade myself you will observe, that they have
" been objects of very great labour & time, every
" ornament & leaf being first made in a separate
" mould, then laid upon the vase with great care &
" accuracy, and afterwards wrought over again upon
" the vase itself by an artist equal to the work ; for
" from the beginning I determined to spare neither
" time nor expence in modelling & finishing my orna-
" ments, and I have the satisfaction to find that my
" plan has hitherto met with the approbation of my
" friends, and that purchasers of every nation declare
" them to be the highest finished & cheapest ornaments
" now made in Europe.—I lamented much that I
" could not obtain liberty of the merchant to send
" a vase, the finest & most perfect I have ever made,[2]
" and which I have since presented to the British
" Museum — It is 18 inches high. Mr. Cha[s] Greville
" saw it, & wished it was in his Majesties cabinet at
" Naples." [3]

The assortment of vases at this time was evidently
large and important, and some must have been of
imposing size, though 18 to 20 inches is the limit of
success in Jasper, and the achievement of this piece
was due to a gradual development.

Notice, too, the standard by which to judge his
work—every ornament and leaf put on separately and

---

[1] Sir William was the Ambassador at Naples at the time.
[2] See illus. facing p. 126.
[3] Letter, Wedgwood to Sir Wm. Hamilton, June 22, 1786.

carefully finished after it was upon the vase by an artist who was equal to the work, and the further assurance that this was the usual plan, which he followed with the approval of his aristocratic patrons ; no scamped work, then, or anything less than the highest finish, must be allowed to pass as the work of this period when every piece had to undergo the censorship of the Master.

The beautiful example of the best period of this class of work, illustrated in colour as the frontispiece to this volume, is in the collection of Her Majesty the Queen. Though not a large piece, only 8 inches high including the pedestal, it has all the features that are looked for and prized by the connoisseur ; the texture is smooth, and gives the impression of velvet to the touch, the colour is the delicate grey blue of the early " bodies " used, the piece being made of this clay, " thrown " upon the wheel, and turned and burnished upon the lathe. There is a slight variation in the tint of the grey blue as between the vase and the pedestal, but this is quite usual, in fact almost universal, when the parts of a vase of this kind have to be fired separately, even though in the same " saggar " the action of the fire will have a different effect upon two pieces standing side by side. The relief decoration is restrained in quantity, and has all the detail and finish associated with the best work. The number of the vase in the old shape book is No. 366, and the date is about 1790. It is undoubtedly a rare piece, possibly unique ; another like it is unknown in any collection.

There is one point that has been mentioned before.

CHAPTER VI

BUSTS AND FIGURES

The artistic quality of basaltes—"Fakes"—Busts and figures
in other colours—Half busts and half figures—Their
uses—Other figures stamped "Wedgwood," but not
Josiah's—The Wedgwoods contemporary with Josiah—
No trace of busts or figures before the days at Etruria—
The start in bust making—The first subjects—Hackwood's valuable work—Orders from Dublin—Variations
and special "things"—Busts of the later period—The
old pricing list for busts—Unique bust of the Rev. Laurence Sterne—Wedgwood's desire to make vases rather
than figures—Figures for candlesticks, lamps, etc.—
Animal figures.

OF all Wedgwood's original work, the section included
under this head presents the most perfect and beautiful
collection. It stands out amongst all his various
achievements as a complete and truly artistic accomplishment. There is not a finer example of the
qualities of his black porcelain, or basaltes, than this;
its highly vitreous nature when fired, and its capability
of acquiring an excellent polish with age and ordinary
daily handling and dusting make it a very real rival
to bronze, for which it has often been mistaken at
first glance. No detail of modelling or minute tool
finishing was lost in the process of firing, and the
extreme hardness of the material rendered it free
from any wearing out or deterioration of surface

either from constant rubbing or the action of damp or atmosphere, it preserved its original texture as when it left the oven, and even after being buried it quickly revives when the surface accumulation of dirt has been washed away.

In the Etruria Museum there is a 6-inch tile of basaltes which had lain in a drain on an old part of the works for probably over a hundred years, and was discovered when foundations for new workshops were being laid; it has the texture and finish that were there when it was first made, uninjured by its long burial in this damp abode.

The opportunity in this class of ware for "fakes" is rare, and collectors should acquire, when the chance offers, any undoubted specimens. They are, as a rule, more perfect because of their hardness, and genuine pieces are frequently found undamaged owing to the fact that they are more free from projecting portions that easily break off from either a blow or a fall than the fragile vases with their delicate handles, lips and feet. The initial expense of production, the cost of models, the necessary finish by the modeller after the model had been acquired to render it suitable for the potter's processes, and the extra care that had to be exercised during the whole routine, have made it less attractive to the imitator than other wares which needed less of the super-handicraft that meant outlay and time, so that rivals and imitators were not so numerous.

Busts and figures were made in other "bodies" besides the basaltes, but not to the same extent; some in "Rosso Antico," in a white terra-cotta,

1. 2.

3. 4.

BLACK BASALTES.

1. BUST OF "PINDAR." 2. BUST OF "BEN JONSON."
3. BUST OF "FLETCHER." 4. BUST OF "HOMER."

(Etruria Museum.)

[To face page 148.

I.

EARTHENWARE.

1. BUST OF " STERNE."

2.   3.

BLACK BASALTES.

2. BUST OF " NEWTON."   3. BUST OF " LOCKE."

(Etruria Museum.)

[*To face page* 149.

and even in cane colour, but few of these exist, though it is possible occasionally to come across them.

An interesting variation is to be found in the half busts and figures [1] which were made at first for the use of architects, but whether made in any quantity or whether they were approved of or used by architects does not appear ; very few remain to-day, and those have been applied to another purpose, viz. as ornaments for the mantelshelf in the same way that one sees brass figures and animals used. These were fixed upon a small foot or pedestal and strengthened at the back, thus forming an ornament which had a front view only. Two figures so treated will be found illustrated. (See illus. facing p. 152.) The surface of these figures and their sharpness of detail were so exquisite, and the production of them so much less expensive than the process of elaborately carving each one in marble—for after the first mould had been obtained reproduction was easy—that Wedgwood, after seeing some Italian chimney pieces, puts forward the suggestion to Bentley : " In my opinion white polish'd " tablets [2] will be liked better for chimney pieces " than any color'd grounds we can made, for they ' will be more like real statuary marble than any ' color'd grounds will be to other stones. What do ' you think of making the figures only in our fine ' white jasper, & let the statuaries put them upon ' their own grounds ? The figures must be contriv'd ' for the purpose & in a large stile, & high relief, ' & so they are carv'd in marble to lay upon the

[1] See illus. facing p. 152.   [2] Marble tablets.

10

that would point to the manufacture of these figures at either of the Burslem Works.

Definite attention was given to bust making about 1770 and 1771, and at first was confined to the antique busts which was found to be much more profitable than figures, but complaint is made of models that had been sent from Mr. Oliver, they were " horrid dear " and of no use to make a mould from—" if you " could borrow some good bronze or marble busts for " us to mold off w^d be the best & cheapest way " ; [1] and a further enlightening remark gives us an idea of the very encouraging help he was able to get from some of his wealthy patrons, " Ld Rockingham has " many Busts wch he w^d lend us at a word, so has " our good fr^d Ld Besbr^o." [2]

His quest for suitable busts was evidently very keen at this time, for he suggests that those at the Academy would be less hackneyed and better for his purpose than those generally supplied by the plaster shops, and to be able to say : " This is from the " Academy, taken from the original in the gallery " etc.," would sound better than that he had it from, Flaxman (a plaster model seller and the father of John Flaxman, R.A.) from whom he supposed they must have what he had got or none at all. He searched everywhere for the best, and let no chance escape of getting it, which is very clearly shown when his selection of models is seen.

During 1774 several plaster models of busts were ordered from Oliver & Hoskins, and these names

[1] Wedgwood to Bentley, February 16, 1771.
[2] *Ibid.*

1 & 2. HALF FIGURES IN CREAM COLOUR, HERCULANEUM SUBJECTS.

(Etruria Museum.)

3. STATUETTE, BASALTES, "VOLTAIRE."

4. STATUETTE, BASALTES, "ROUSSEAU."

(Wedgwood Institute, Burslem.)

[*To face page* 152.

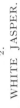

1. 2. 3.

WHITE JASPER.

1. STATUETTE, "JUPITER," ON COLOURED JASPER PEDESTAL, WITH RELIEF DECORATION.
2. STATUETTE, "JUPITER," ON COLOURED JASPER PEDESTAL, WITH RELIEF DECORATION.

are given : Homer,[1] large and small, Solon, Pindar,[2] Plato, Epicurus, Zeno, Minerva, Venus, Palladio, Inigo Jones, Junius Brutus, Marcus Brutus, Agrippina, Seneca, Antinous, Faustina, Augustus Cæsar, Antonius Pius, Marcus Aurelius, Germanicus, Cato. In reference to these, about a month later we read : " We " are going on with the Busts, but we proceed very " slowly, it being a fortnight's work to repair & mould " one of these heads, & whilst this business continues " we have no body to work at the Statues." [3] But the next information received after about one month's further work has been bestowed upon them is that they are going on very fast, as they are having four of the principal hands on the works constantly at work upon them. " You will find our Busts much " finer, & better finish'd than the Plaister ones we " take them from—Hackwood bestows abo^t a week " upon each head in restoring it to what we suppose " it was when it came out of the hands of the " Statuary." [4] The earnestness with which this new section of work was attacked fully coincides with the rest of his indefatigable and persistent methods, for Hackwood, whose work was becoming all-important and indispensable, was so busy upon them that other work for which he was needed could not be undertaken, and the reason given in December of this year is : " The Busts will employ him for a year or two " before our collection is tolerably complete, & I am " much set upon having it so, being fully perswaded

---

[1] See illus. facing p. 148.   [2] See illus. facing p. 148.
[3] Wedgwood to Bentley, July 21, 1774.
[4] Wedgwood to Bentley, August 16, 1774.

" they will be a capital article with us, & Hackwood
" finishes them admirably.   They are infinitely superior
" to the Plaister ones we take them from, as you will
" see more fully when you come to Etruria.   I hope
" in time to send you a collection of the finest Heads
" in this World." [1]

The year was a busy one in this section : some very
small busts, Voltaires, etc., are promised to London,
with some larger, and this time in white composition,
not the black basaltes—a promise that was fulfilled
during the year, some being sent " finished, & fired,
" & very good " for Bentley's approval, asking how
many shall be made and whether the fluted pedestal
upon which they are placed is suitable, or too thick,
or too large.

These details of the manufacture and dates of the
appearance of first specimens are given because it is
thought that they may help each individual to an
opinion and decision about any piece before him, and
also because this manufacturing side of the question
has not been emphasised before.   That it holds the
solution of many a difficulty goes without saying and
it is hoped will assist those for whom this volume is
intended.

The introduction of these busts called forth an
immediate demand, and requests for fresh subjects
seem to have worried those who were already so fully
occupied at bust making.   From Dublin the demand
came from a titled source for George III, King William,
and Henry IV of France, all life size, with the information, " these will sell well in Dublin," but caution

[1] Wedgwood to Bentley, September 11, 1774.

is shown in Wedgwood's remarks to Bentley : " Shall
" we make them ? " " Are there any to be got in
" plaister ? " That this was the period when most of
the busts were made, we know from the continual
reference to them in letters, and the reassuring information : " Statues & Busts are in the making "—
" Homer & Shakespear are made," which points to the
constant inquiries that must have been received from
London for them.

There is difficulty to-day in naming some of the
portraits, and it is interesting to come upon a note
which tells of a similar difficulty existing then, as
when a question arises : " We are at a loss about
" the Solon Bust order'd, having no other Solon than
" what we have called Demosthenes. He holds his
" head on one side something like the Roman Grinder,
" you know the Bust very well—Mr. Cox says it was
" called Solon when it first came here in Plaister, &
" continues under that name in our Catalogue — We
" shall send you one or two of these." [1]

Dublin proved a good market for these busts, for
Mr. Brock (Wedgwood's agent at Dublin) orders
freely, as one item alone will show : " Mr. Brock
" has sent us a noble order for busts. Not less than
" 105." [2] By this time the list must have been very
nearly complete, and there seems to have been no
serious difficulty to prevent the even flow of
production.

Variations, new methods of utilizing the material
at hand, were always being suggested at Etruria,

[1] Wedgwood to Bentley, May 7, 1777.
[2] *Ibid.*, November 8, 1778.

and approval was continually being solicited upon the latest ideas for the improvement of any of the designs and models that were at this time literally pouring out from the studios and workshops. Special " things " were continually placed in the boxes that found their way regularly to London. " You will " find a few things in this box which you have not " seen before, along with some Garrick heads which " you wanted, a head of Voltaire in white Jasper, " upon a Basalte Pedastal Richly ornamented with " the disconsolate muse, her Lyre unstrung at her " feet & other suitable insignia, upon the death of so " great a man." [1]

Some well-known busts, which have been added since the first Wedgwood's time and cannot obviously belong to an old Wedgwood collection, have in some cases found their way there ; they are beautiful specimens of basaltes in many cases, but not belonging to " the period."

Many of these were introduced about 1850, and Wyon, the sculptor, was responsible for several of them. They included Wesley, Watt, the two Stephensons, Tennyson, Palmerston, Campbell, and Bunyan. Of course Wesley and Watt could have been contemporary, but the Wedgwood busts of these were not.

The illustration given from a photograph of the original pricing list for the figure maker (potter) shows four of the large busts which were made (but these are not known to exist in basaltes) ; the moulds or portions of them are still at Etruria.

[1] Wedgwood to Bentley, December 5, 1778.

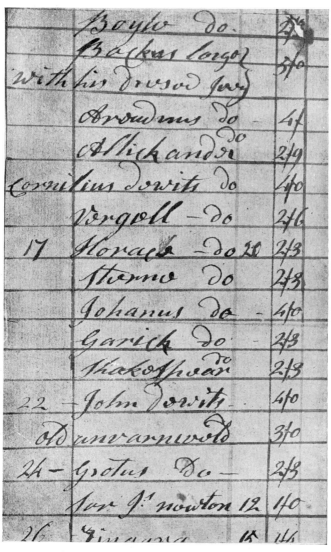

	Boyle do.	4/
	Backus longer	3/6
with his dress jury		
	Andrews do	4/
	Allichander do	2/9
Cornilius dowits do		4/0
	Virgell do	2/6
17	Horace do 20	2/3
	Thomo do	2/3
	Johanus do	4/0
	Garick do	2/3
	Thackspear do	2/3
22	John Dowits	4/0
	Old unvarnised	3/0
24	Grotus Do	2/3
	Sar Js newton 12	1/0
26	Virginia 15	1/6

PART OF A PAGE FROM THE OLD PRICING BOOK, SHOWING BUSTS.
(Etruria Museum.)

[*To face page* 156.

1 & 2. PAIR OF CANDLESTICKS IN BLUE AND WHITE JASPER.

3. FIGURE CANDLESTICK, JASPER, "CYBELE."

4. FIGURE CANDLESTICK, JASPER, "CERES."

(Etruria Museum.)

It is certain that these were made, as a price has been fixed for the making of them, a thing that was never done until there had been actual production.

The bust of the Rev. Laurence Sterne appears among them, and the only one known to exist is made in earthenware bisque and is in the Etruria Museum. An illustration is shown. (See illus. facing p. 149.)

The four busts referred to above are :—

Bacchus
Ariadne
Alexander
Sterne

The spelling and writing are both interesting.

The statues were not very numerous, but some of them were amongst the earliest of ornamental pieces introduced to give a contrast and variety to the mantelshelves and cabinets along with the Etruscan vases which are first mentioned as early as 1769 [1] in connection with the Etruscan earth (or basaltes). At this time there was also voiced a distinct disapproval about the " painted " figures, which were evidently allowed to occupy positions in the best houses, for the reason, no doubt, that better were not available, and the hope is entertained that the figures which he was collecting and proposing to make in black would cause a revolution in taste, and be fitting companions to his Etruscan vases, which were then in high favour. Conditions at the works and the state of orders were so satisfactory that haste in this matter was not advisable, and the usual careful

[1] See illus. facing p. 115.

thought and consideration was brought to bear upon this new venture. It is evident that the first suggestion about making figures had not altogether received the approval of his partner, for that idea is lurking in Wedgwood's mind when he replies to some reference of Bentley's to black figures : " I have not seen " these s^d black figures which have converted you " again to a good Opinion of figure making, therefore " if I sho^d waver a little you will not wonder." [1] However, not wishing to let the matter drop, he continues to probe the question still further, and offers reasons why they should not be too hasty, yet at the same time cannot conceal his desire to enter upon it, as shown in the last sentence of the paragraph, which looks to a source from which they could get assistance if it was decided to commence upon the work. " My opinion is, that if we make more Vases " than will be sold, or, find hands, who can make " figures, & cannot work at Vases, then we sho^d set " about figure making, but 'till one of these cases " happen I cannot help thinking our hands are better " imploy'd at Vases. If there was any such thing as " getting one sober figure maker to bring up some " Boys I sho^d like to ingage in that branch. Suppose " you inq^r at Bow, I despair of any at Derby." [2]

After this the matter was not allowed to rest, for it comes up among other items in the correspondence at intervals, yet very little progress seems to have been made until about six years later. Then we find mention of two Muses " model'd Statue size " ; one was Terpsichore, received from Sir Roger Newdigate,

[1] Wedgwood to Bentley, November 19, 1769.　　[2] *Ibid.*

and the other was modelled in London. An Infant Hercules upon a pedestal is also mentioned, and another reference to two sizes of the small statues : " Hercules, & Piping Faun, &c. are one size—The " Vestal, Esculapius, &c. are a size larger." [1]

The statue of Voltaire which is so well known was taken from a model that arrived on the works from London in July 1777, and a promise is given that copies shall be made of it, but " it will not be in the waxen composition." Several of these Voltaire statues were sent later in the year in black upon a pedestal, and this is the colour in which they were generally made, although some with the figure of Rousseau as a companion were in cane colour. These latter were not very satisfactory, as they were much discoloured in burning, although every precaution had been observed : " We covered them close in burning knowing " how apt this body is to turn brown, but in vain." [2]

In the original set there were also the following figures :—

Neptune, 2 feet high.
Triton, 2 feet high.
Polyphemus, 19 inches × 16 inches.
Morpheus, a reclining figure, 25 inches long.
Ceres, a sitting figure.
Ganymede, from the Florentine Museum, 12 inches.
Bacchus, from Sansovino, 11 inches.
Bacchus, from Michael Angelo, 11 inches.
Bacchus (another), 10¾ inches.
Faun, 10¾ inches.

[1] Wedgwood to Bentley, May 23, 1777.
[2] *Ibid.*, October 16, 1779.

Apollo, 11 inches.

Mercury, 11 inches.

Venus (Medici), 10½ inches.

Venus, rising from the sea, upon a pedestal richly ornamented with figures, representing the Seasons, 6½ inches.

Several have been added since the first period, some being of very recent date.

Other very finely modelled figures, chiefly female, were adapted to candlesticks and lamps, forming pieces of ornamental ware, and not statues.[1]

Sphinxes, lions, tritons, and griffins were used separately on plinths to form paper weights, or fitted with nozzles to hold tapers for sealing, or candles for lighting purposes.

Two pug dogs and two elephants belong to the first series, but these are rare and must not be confused with the modern models in basaltes from the same factory.

[1] See illus. facing p. 157.

VII

TABLETS
MEDALLIONS
CAMEOS
INTAGLIOS

CHAPTER VII

TABLETS, MEDALLIONS, CAMEOS, INTAGLIOS

The period covered by this class—The zeal and originality given to its production—The variety of subjects chosen—Wedgwood's opinion of tablet making—The personal element—The advantage of Jasper over marble—Its value and price—Tablets in red and black—Success dated—An original list of subjects—Flaxman's model—Appreciation of efforts—White Jasper tablets—The cameo series—Royal Patronage and portrait medallions—The adaptation of cameos to seals—Their introduction into various articles of use and ornament—The earlier cameos with enamel grounds—Intaglios—Different ways of mounting the same—Historical cabinets—The Sydney Cove cameo—Extracts from Governor Phillips' letters—The slave cameo—Memorial cameos for Germany—Introduction of cameos into jewellery—Portrait medallions—Illustrious moderns—The classical sets—Flaxman's contribution to the series—Hackwood's share—Admiral Keppel—Dr. Priestley—Sir Isaac Newton—Sir Wm. Hamilton.

AMONG the products of Wedgwood's energies this section, included in the original catalogue under Classes I to XI, covers the longest range, extending over almost the whole of his career as a potter, from the early Burslem days until his death, for to the completing and perfecting of this his attention never flagged.

It was for this primarily that he made his Jasper

" body," and went to the tedious process of trying every likely material which he came across. It has been said that he was without the knowledge of a chemist, and it is quite possible that such chemical knowledge as he could then have obtained would have hindered rather than helped. The method that he used, coupled with the careful recording of every unexpected variation under actual treatment, proved more useful to him than much theory. It has often been found by potters that after some supposed scientific method has failed success may be achieved by " rule of thumb." Perhaps this is because the one requires exceptional exactness of conditions and the other is able to disregard such niceties and by sheer luck perhaps surmount all obstacles.

Without commenting further upon this, it is certain that it was only after many failures that Wedgwood attained success, and this success was built up by continual experimenting, much deliberation and de-duction—all agree there never was his equal as an experimenter. His results were at the time quite original, such as were not being sought after by others, until his recipes leaked out and were used by imitators ; yet still his tablets, medallions, and cameos stood foremost in his day, and have continued to do so until the present time. No one tried to give to the world what he did, the infinite variety of subjects in small gems, cameos, and intaglios, which were produced in thousands for every use that jewellery or ornamentation could suggest, and the marvellous gallery of portraits, in all sizes, of ancient and modern illustrious men and women.

His large pieces, tablets for inlaying in walls or chimney pieces, or for framing as pictures, were made rectangular, oval and other shapes, in all sizes, and represent the outcome of years of battling with and overcoming difficulties of materials, workmanship, and firing, standing out as a great achievement. When one examines these exquisite specimens, from an artistic as well as a technical standpoint, the question presents itself, Are there any other products to compare with them in material so suitable, in texture so beautiful, in subject so simply interpreted, so technically perfect, so permanent, and so cheap ? Similar subjects produced by almost any other means in marble, wood, metal, are more costly and have not the permanency of Jasper, nor do they possess a higher finish.

The first tablets that we know date about 1770 and include some of large-size Herculaneum figures in circular frames made in one piece and in a cream, buff, or red hard terra-cotta " body," often bronzed in the same manner as some of the Etruscan vases. As with every other successful innovation, the demand always came in excess of the ability to supply, which is made known in the reply which had often to be sent : " We have no Tablets ready at present." This referred to white and fawn coloured, the white being cream colour, as the Jasper " body " had not then been introduced. Four of these fine tablets are shown in the illustrations facing p. 121.

These were pressed in a mould, the figures not being applied separately as in the case of the Jasper and Basaltes which were of a later date. The latter

11

were referred to as being in a " new vein " which
was started in 1772, and caused some amount of
trouble in making them exact to certain sizes which
had evidently been given by those who wanted them
to fit into an existing chimney piece. " We will make
" the black Tablets for Lady Wynne as near to size
" as we can & the Glass grinders must do the rest
" as we cannot command the accidents which cause
" our clay to sink more or less to the ⅛th of an inch.
" I think we may make a few more of the same sizes,
" as they are the proper ones for Chimney pieces, &
" that being the case I think it follows that out of
" all our variety of Bassreliefs we have not one of a
" proper size for the Tablet of a Chimney piece, in
" which form they certainly stand the best chance of
" being sold." [1] Here is certain ground upon which
to give the date at which the search for suitable
subjects and sizes for the making of these tablets
begins. Here the same story has to be told again,
failure alternating with success and disappointment
once more : " We have made eight Tablets at different
" times for Sr W. W^s [2] & all bad, it is so long and
" narrow we cannot keep them straight. . . . We will
" try again but I despair of success." [3] And this
continues for some time as the only reference made
during the next year is to the effect that " the black
" Tablets we cannot manage cleverly." [4]

However, during this silence much must have been
accomplished, for the conqueror's voice is unmistakable

[1] Wedgwood to Bentley, September 13, 1772.
[2] Sir Watkin Wynne.
[3] Wedgwood to Bentley, November 15, 1772.
[4] Ibid., January 2, 1773.

in the sentence : " Tablet making is the nicest branch
" of our business & requires a longer series of my
" attention, & real working at them than I can possibly
" give them without being broke in upon, & interupted
" & that spoils the whole. Oh ! for more time, &
" less interuption." [1] The uphill work which all this
meant can be imagined ; all hands had to be trained,
a slow process, and all new departures were delayed.
When this is realised, how much more interesting
and valuable do all these early pieces become, for it
is evident that every piece had the individual attention of the Master himself often in a very practical
form. Here is another note which will give some
insight into the working of these tablets when they
were in their early stages : " Our Fish drain maker,
" at the Usefull works, has been trying his hand at
" long square Tablets for 2 months past, & has made
" some tolerable good ones which we shall polish &
" send you, but they will be rather for Pictures than
" Chimney pieces." [2] The wonder is that such excellence was attained ; it is seldom that an old piece
falls short of the high standard aimed at.

There is always something about a piece of ware
which convinces one at once of its genuineness, apart
entirely from the mark. To many the former is the
surest test. The personal element which entered so
largely into all the early stages of the various new
wares that were made will, indeed, account for this,
for otherwise it is certain deterioration in standard
would soon have commenced. The frequent messages

---

[1] Wedgwood to Bentley, August 22, 1774.
[2] *Ibid.*, November 6, 1774.

that came from the partner in London, spurring up and putting the works upon its mettle, had a stimulating effect, which is seen in such words as the following : " I observe the stress you lay upon having " Tablets made of a proper size & form for Chimney " pieces, & the consequence it is likely to be of having " tried all the hands I have who were likely to execute " them, but in vain, I have taken the business up " myself, & am not much afraid of being able to " complete it to your satisfaction." [1]

The making of these tablets still gave much trouble, and success as yet was only partial ; the verdict upon them was that they " are pretty good —   They have " been 5 or 6 weeks in drying & burning —   Cost some " Guineas Modelling & moulding, & are very bad " things to make." [2]

Many plain tablets in black basaltes were made for Bentley and went to London to have figure subjects painted upon them, and these seem to have met with great success : " The fame of your painted " chimney piece is not confin'd to London only. We " are asked much after them here, and if you can " spare us a good sett to shew here this summer now " our season is commenc'd it will be a treat at least " to our visitants if we do not sell them, but I think " the latter is very probable, & I have almost promis'd " this treat to some of our constant friends & cus- " tomers here." [3]

The mastery over long tablets had not come in

[1] Wedgwood to Bentley, January 14, 1775.
[2] *Ibid.*, February 6, 1775.
[3] *Ibid.*, July 8, 1775.

PLACQUE, JASPER; SUBJECT, "THE BIRTH OF BACCHUS."

PLACQUE, WHITE JASPER; SUBJECT, "THE MUSES."

PLACQUE, BLUE AND WHITE JASPER, "DANCING HOURS,"
BY FLAXMAN.

(Etruria Museum.)

[*To face page* 168.

I.

I. LARGE OVAL PLACQUE IN BLACK BASALTES; SUBJECT,
"BACCHUS AND PANTHER."

(Etruria Museum.)

2.   3.

2. PLACQUE, JASPER, ANTIQUE FIGURE AND GREYHOUND.
3. PLACQUE, JASPER, SACRIFICE FIGURE.

(Wedgwood Institute, Burslem.)

[To face page 169.

1776 ; a note saying that the two tablets of " The Birth of Bacchus " and " The Triumph of Bacchus," which were being modelled especially by Hackwood, could not be attempted in one continuous tablet ; the suggestion is made that they should be made to fill " A Frise very cleverly in separate pieces." A drawing is given showing five ovals, the figures white and the grounds blue, all the pieces together making up the subject and filling the chimney piece frieze better than a series of detached single figures having no connection with each other. This is the first step from the plain tablet with painted subject and the basaltes basrelief tablet to the Jasper tablet with white figures and coloured ground, but this had not actually appeared, though soon after one may safely conclude that some few pieces were attempted and came out good from the oven amongst a larger proportion that were bad. " You will judge better than " I can what the Tablet, Birth of Bacchus, ought to " be charged, by comparing it with other things. " Gent^n may, & will pay more for a Tablet than for " a mere Picture. These with color'd grounds are " difficult & expensive to make & should be sold " accordingly. It is harder, finer, & better work'd " than Marble, & what would it cost in that material." [1] The whole question of this tablet making was one of dogged application which was entered upon with the determination to succeed. The feeling that the successes should be made to pay for the failures shows that the latter must have been pretty heavy, and the former sufficiently good to command a high price ;

[1] Wedgwood to Bentley, February 21, 1776.

in fact, technique and workmanship were evidently satisfactory, and it only remained a matter of firing that caused the loss : " You will receive a Tablet, " the only one which has stood free from cracking " in cooling out of four, So that you must put a " tolerable price upon the living, or the dead will " not be paid for. The Tablet of Silenus, if it had " been whole, would have been worth 4 or 5 Guineas, " Nothing so fine can be had for five times the " money, if at all, & these things can only be had " from us, nor shall we have any competitors in " haste." [1]

The trouble and loss which these fine products caused was very tantalising, for no sooner was the summit reached than by a sudden descent the valley again became the camping ground where the heights could be clearly viewed, but to reach them the weary process of slow climbing had to be commenced again, and the despondent note is once more heard when only six months later we read : " We will make no " more Tablets 'till we have farther orders, & I appre- " hend we never shall make a Perfect one. Very " few fine large things are perfect. Perhaps none." [2]

The making of tablets for chimney pieces was not, however, discontinued, but was diverted to red, or red upon black, or black bronzed, and these were supplied with the information that all the " appen- " dages " to these could be made in Jasper, that is small ovals to go with them, but the tablets themselves, being large pieces, must have a different fire, or the

[1] Wedgwood to Bentley, May 29, 1776.
[2] *Ibid.*, November 16, 1776.

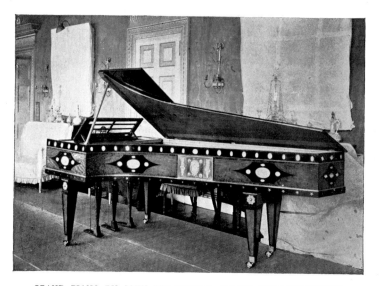

GRAND PIANO BY JOHN BROADWOOD, INLAID WITH WEDGWOOD
CAMEOS AND TASSIE GEMS.

[To face page 170.

PLACQUE ; SUBJECT, "THE MARRIAGE OF CUPID AND PSYCHE"
JASPER, MOUNTED IN ORMOLU GILT FRAME.

PLACQUE ; SUBJECT, "SACRIFICE TO HYMEN"; JASPER,
MOUNTED IN ORMOLU GILT FRAME.

(From the private collection of H.M. The Queen.)

[*To face page 171.*

composition must be adapted, " either of which may
" possibly be a work of some time, or it may not.
" I have trials for the latter purpose in almost every
" kiln." So hope was always in the ascendant, and
to confidence of ultimate success we owe the much-
coveted specimens of large placques which we have
to-day.

A year later, at the end of 1777, when it was evident
that some of the difficulties had been overcome,
preparations were in hand to make and fire some
large tablets, but no promise was given that sizes
could be guaranteed, as only future experiments could
determine that point.

Encouragement was not lacking, and Wedgwood
was urged on by the constant applications for them
and the actual orders that were received, to which
the reply invariably was that they would be attempted.

The date at which success came must be placed
about a year later still, viz. August 1778, for then
we have a record of the subjects and sizes that already
existed and a question raised as to what it was necessary
to make to complete the show for the next winter
season in London. It is a halting place where some
very definite details can be noted which show how
much had been accomplished towards perfecting the
tablets that were shortly to be produced. " We are
" making jasper tablets for your next winters shew.
" I will repeat to you the sorts we have at present
" that you may consider if the variety will be suffi-
" cient, or we should have more modeled, & likewise
" what number you have in London of each & what
" addition we shall make to complete your assortment.

" Marr^e of C. & P.   5 sizes large inough for tablets.
"   We are making 2 of each.
" Dancing hours for tablets or frises. We have abo^t
"   6 made with those sent lately & shall stop
"   for farther orders. We have two tablets,
"   making 12 hours of these.
" Etruscan, with Homer, &c. We have made 2 &
"   shall wait for orders.
" Apollo & the 9 Muses in two frises to accompany
"   the above, or to be used as separate tablets.
"   2 of each made.
" Choice of Hercules. 3 or 4 sizes. We wait farther
"   orders.
" Triumph of Bacchus, largest with attending Fauns,
"   &c.— Shall wait.
" Birth of do. — do. with   do. —   do.
" Boys & Goat largest. Has only been made in red
"   but is a good thing.   Shall wait your orders.
" Sacrifice to Flora —   New & large. We have sold
"   one & shall make two more.
" Do.   to Bacchus. New, very large. We shall
"   make two of them.

" The above 12 sorts of large tablets will make a
" pretty good assortment & most of them are new.
" We propose to make one other, The triumph of
" Ariadne, & will then follow your directions." [1]

This truly chronicles success ; confidence and
assurance are the dominant notes. " We shall make "
and " We have made " leave no doubt upon the
subject, and it may safely be taken that this is the
period when tablets made their appearance as ap-

[1] Wedgwood to Bentley, August 19, 1778.

proved and perfect pieces. The enlightening extract given above follows hard upon a letter which prepares the way for it, and evidently refers to the stock of red and black tablets which were in London and which it would be advisable to dispose of before this new " shew " was introduced. The opening sentence refers to the new jasper tablets, and what follows is a display of legitimate jubilation :   " Do you wish to " have any tablets sent ? or would you rather sell " what you have first ?   We have a perfect one from " Mr. Flaxman's model, & have several more in hand " of different subjects.   You shall have a most glorious " assortment for the opening of the next season, of " Tablets, frises & blocks to go together in the com- " position of a chimney piece.   We can make frises " of any length & very true & even.

" I have just mixed near half a ton of Jasper, & " shall go on with more that we may have a year's " composition beforehand, the advantage of which " will be very great in many respects ; & when we " have completed our present suit of tablets & their " accompaniments for chimney pieces we will make " another attack upon the architects & hope to " conquer.   One thing I am at least clear in, that " our weapons will be superior to any we have hitherto " brandish'd before them." [1]

These gentlemen were, at least some of them, " converted to the true belief in our tablets " ; although the process was a slow one, it was sure in the end, and the very best efforts of Etruria were put forward for that purpose.

[1] Wedgwood to Bentley, August 9, 1778.

Tablets in white jasper upon a white jasper ground
were made for this purpose, and very fine pieces they
proved to be ; they called from Wedgwood the remark : " The white Jasper muses, & tablet of Homer
" & Hesiod are worth any thing. Please to look at
" them, & if you think they should be charged less
" than the blue grounds, put them at what you please.
" These very fine & perfect works should be charg'd
" singly, upon inspection, with some relation to their
" individual merit—& where the merit of such large
" pieces as tablets, or such suits as the muses rise
" above a medium, I think they should be mark'd
" with a price accordingly. What I mean to offer to
" your consideration upon this subject is shortly this.
" That a Homer & Hesiod tablet, or a suit of muses
" should not have a fixed, & invariable price like a
" quart mug, but that this individual tablet or that
" suit of muses should be so much—8. 10. or 12 G⁸.
" according to their comparative merit & if it is
" necessary to fix a medium price, I would never-
" theless have some fixed both above & below that
" medium if the difference in the fineness of the pieces
" would bear the distinction." ¹ Not many of these
remain ; one of the " Muses " tablets, a " Bacchus
and Panther " ² and a single figure are in the Museum
at Etruria. The first named will be seen in the
illustration.

The cameos of Wedgwood and Bentley form a very
complete collection of various sets of subjects, taken
from the finest antique gems and adapted for setting

¹ Wedgwood to Bentley, March 15, 1779.
² In Basaltes, see illus. facing p. 169.

in rings, lockets, and bracelets or mounted as buttons. Made in the jasper coloured bodies they were as durable as any imitations could be, were cheaper than any other form, and much sharper than those in glass. This series was also made in intaglio form for seals; the list is a very long one, over 600, comprising Egyptian history, gods and goddesses, and sacrifices. The ancient kings, philosophers, poets, orators, the fabulous age of the Greeks, the War of Troy, and Roman history, are also represented by about 700 more, about 20 masks, chimeras, etc. Some illustrious men and an appendix which was added to the catalogue of 1779 brought the number up to 1,700. As these in the original sets of intaglios were impressed with number as well as name, they are easily recognised. Many of them have a good polish upon the ground, leaving the figure untouched, and in the case of the shank seals, the shank was polished as well as the bezel and ground of the intaglio itself. Some also had blue jasper grounds, making them resemble exactly the black and blue onyxes which were so much used for seal cutting.

The start in this branch could not have been made before there was a capable artist on the works; Hackwood was the first that was engaged. The date of the letter which contains the first reference to these products may well be taken as the time when they were sufficiently perfect to be offered for sale. This was at the time when the productions of Etruria received royal interest and patronage, and the suggestion was made that their Majesties' portraits should be modelled for reproduction as medallions. Hackwood had already tried his "novice" hand at a portrait of the son and heir of Mrs. Crewe, and over this transaction there is mention of gems such as Cupid and Psyche, etc., or a favourite head, for setting into snuffbox tops. (See illus. facing p. 189.)

This was in 1771, about two years after settling in the new works at Etruria, and there was evidently some demand for them, as the following year we hear of "a variety of Gems & other things in the "bisket oven," and the preparing of "all the bas- "reliefs we have that are capable of such a meta- "morphasis to be converted into Cameos, by clearing "& smoothing the back grounds." [1] In entering upon this work the same careful attention to detail was observed, advice sought as to the best way to make them, so as to produce them in the form most acceptable to customers, whether flat grounds, concave or convex would be preferred, how they should be mounted, etc., and a score of other queries which would help in the making of an article that would supply a need or create a sale. Many were mounted in metal, metal gilt and in gold, both as rings and bracelets, and these methods of introducing them into jewellery found great favour. They sold well mounted into tortoiseshell boxes, and were also put into pedestals for vases and candlesticks.

As buttons for sleeves, cloaks and ladies' dresses they were made in great quantities, and in the early days before the jasper colours were introduced a great many of these cameos were made in white, the background being coloured in with water colour

[1] Wedgwood to Bentley, March 28, 1772.

and then mounted under crystal by the button makers and box makers, Wedgwood himself remarking that they looked much better that way than his own burnt in enamel grounds, and being covered with glass, they were sufficiently durable. The great desire to get these beautiful gems noticed in the highest places led to the making of some in the Cherokee clay, to be shown to their Majesties, and this again led to their introduction to many others, till the sale seems to have been highly satisfactory.

The Cherokee clay was used in the jasper and other " bodies." It was a special material and was the object of a journey to South Carolina in 1767 and 1768, undertaken by Mr. T. Griffiths, brother of Dr. Griffiths of the *Monthly Review*, at Wedgwood's request.

In 1773 it was still being used for the finest pieces : " I am preparing some of the Cherokee Clay for Gems " and Cameo's, & when you have finish'd some of " them & got a good collection of them, Black Onyxes— " Polish'd Seals &c I could wish you by all means to " wait upon their Majestys." [1]

At a later date the supply seems to have been stopped : " I have often thought of mentioning to " you that it may not be a bad idea to give out, that " our jaspers are made of the Cherokee clay which " I sent an agent into that country on purpose to " procure for me, & when the present parcel is out " we have no hopes of obtaining more, as it was with " the utmost difficulty the natives were prevail'd " upon to part with what we now have, though

[1] Wedgwood to Bentley, November 21, 1773.

" recommended to them by their father Stuart,[1]
" Intendant of Indian affairs. But then his Majesty
" should see some of these large fine tablets, & be
" told this story (which is a true one for I am not
" Joking) the first, as he has repeatedly enquir'd
" what I have done with the Cherokee clay." [2]

Cameos in two, three, or more colours were made
for introduction into special pieces of furniture, such
as cabinets, bureaux, commodes, and at the time of
the introduction of the Grand Pianoforte the case
lent itself admirably to the introduction of fine medallions and cameos in its decoration.

In the year 1796 an instrument with this decoration
was made by John Broadwood, upon which no pains
or cost were spared. Its historic interest and beauty,
as well as the fact that it is still in existence in splendid
preservation—the satinwood mellowed with age, the
keys unworn and the medallions perfect—is sufficient
reason for this reference to it.

It was made to the order of Don Manuel de Godoy
(Prince of the Peace), and was presented by him to
Queen Maria Louisa of Spain.

It took four months to make, and was delivered at
the Bull, Porters Galley Quay, for the Esperanza,
Belotte, Bilbao.

The design for this instrument is preserved by the
maker, but the piano itself was unknown for years,
until the early part of this century, when a Parisian
dealer in antiquities wrote to an English lady about

---

[1] James Stuart (1700–1779) accompanied General Oglethorpe to
America. He was appointed general agent and superintendent of
Indian affairs in 1763, and was much beloved by the Indians.

[2] Wedgwood to Bentley, December 15, 1777.

PLACQUE ; SUBJECT, " SACRIFICE FIGURE " ; JASPER, MOUNTED
IN ORMOLU GILT FRAME.

PLACQUE; SUBJECT, " ANTONIA AND URN " ; JASPER, MOUNTED
IN ORMOLU GILT FRAME.

(From the private collection of H.M. The Queen.)

[*To face page* 178.

1.   2.

1. PORTRAIT MEDALLION, "GEORGE III," BY HACKWOOD, JASPER,
    MOUNTED IN ORMOLU GILT FRAME.
2. PORTRAIT MEDALLION, "QUEEN CHARLOTTE," BY HACKWOOD,
    JASPER, MOUNTED IN ORMOLU GILT FRAME.

3.   4.

3. PORTRAIT MEDALLION, ' SHAKESPEARE," BY HACKWOOD, JASPER,
    MOUNTED IN ORMOLU GILT FRAME.
4. PORTRAIT MEDALLION, "CAPTAIN COOK," BY FLAXMAN, JASPER.

(From the private collection of H.M. The Queen.)

[*To face page* 179.

it, with the result that it is now in an English drawing-room. Probably it was looted from Spain in the Napoleonic Wars and remained unknown but well cared for, most likely in some French château.

The cost is fully set out as follows :—

The Count Mopox Grenier's Hotel. D.̃

A Grand Pianoforte 6 octaves C to C. in sattinwood case ornamented with different woods with water gilt mouldings and Wedgwood's and Tassie's medallions, etc., The Prince of Peace's arms chased and gilt in burnished gold rich carved frame, etc.	£223	13	0
The Prince's portrait in front by Taylor.	10	10	0
A Cover of green striped Leather and stockings for the legs.	9	9	0
A Green baize Cover.	1	7	0
A Deal case very stout for the Instr.	5	10	0
A do. do. frame.	5	7	0
Strings, forks, etc.	1	1	0
Cartage to the Key.	0	7	6
	£257	4	6

An illustration is shown of this Broadwood piano inlaid with cameos. (See illus. facing p. 170.)

Another way of using them was as little cameo pictures framed in metal bezels, making choice miniature pieces for the decoration of ladies' dressing-rooms, and in this form they went into the foreign market. Catalogues and pattern cards were printed both in French and Italian as well as English, and about this time, 1773, probably all cameos and intaglios would be impressed with name and identification number.

Up to the end of 1773 all the gems and cameos were either white or buff with coloured enamel grounds which were burnt in, although, as we have seen, many customers who bought them to apply to their own purposes, coloured the grounds in with colours which were not vitrified. Then a definite period came with the introduction and perfecting of the coloured jasper bodies, which were applied to these gems and cameos, and gradually, as far as Wedgwood & Bentley were concerned, became the customary product. Some experimental attempts to enamel the jasper cameos were successful, but whether this process was used at all is not easy to determine.

The pre-1774 series is a very beautiful one, and not many specimens are to be found now, so that any that may appear should be acquired. They will form a collection entirely distinct from the later Jasper series.

It is interesting to note the issue of the double cameo and double intaglio which are comparatively scarce now. The idea was undoubtedly suggested by the fact that the metal mounters used to put two of the single ones back to back when mounting them and so form an ornament that had, so to speak, two fronts, and a seal which could have two subjects instead of one. Wedgwood made many of these double pieces, both as cameos and seals. There was, of course, no space on which to stamp the name; still the connoisseur should have no difficulty in being able to tell them when they present themselves.

Fewer still are the double pieces, generally made in pale blue jasper having the intaglio upon the one side and the cameo of the same subject in white upon the other. Those that we have seen undoubtedly belong to the best period of Jasper, and are always of most excellent technique. The difficulty of "placing" these small pieces for the oven so that each side could receive the necessary action of the oven atmosphere adds a further interest to them, for jasper must be exposed to the direct action of the atmosphere of the oven to give it both colour and texture.

One specimen that would be worth finding has George III on one side and Queen Charlotte on the other, and Wedgwood specially asks about this in a letter to Bentley, at the same time mentioning "Omphale," "The Conquer'd Province," "Hercules strangling the Nemean lion," and a few such high relief figures. "If you have any favorite heads for "this purpose pray name them as we shall have them "in hand in a few days." [1]

In examining these minute pieces of work one is struck with the delicate nature of the modelling and the skill and patience required to prepare them. We are told that the one who was entrusted with this work, probably the only one, was Hackwood, who "has more necessary work before him in repairing "& raising good bass-reliefs which now lie useless "amongst our stores, Thickening seals for polishing

[1] Wedgwood to Bentley, April 16, 1777.

12

" &c. &c. than he can go thro' in 12 months without
" putting him to any original modelling. These
" things he does admirably & is most usefully employ'd
" in them." [1]

Every likely source of supply for fresh or new
subjects was eagerly watched; indeed, the collection
was increased whenever an opportunity offered.

The desire to make these cameos suitable for
different markets and purposes was very keen, and
they were introduced into the wholesale channel
among manufacturers of all classes of bric-à-brac in
wood, metal, tortoiseshell, etc., for boxes, cases and
small furniture.

Some cameos received very special treatment, and
much time and care were expended upon them so
as to render them fit subjects for introducing into
the " tops of gold boxes, but of all the modes of dis-
" posing of cameos that of making them up into little
" Historical Cabinets seems to me the most likely to
" make them worthy of notice." [2]

One of the most beautiful cameos made originally
in clay that was sent by Sir Joseph Banks from Sydney
Cove [3] has been somewhat plentifully reproduced in
coloured jasper bodies since the first were made.
Two hundred of the original cameos were sent out to
the new colony to Governor Phillips and may very
well have been " all the first " mentioned in Wedgwood's letter to Dr. Darwin, but with the exception
of one only, which the author saw in Sydney in 1914,

[1] Wedgwood to Bentley, October 27, 1777.

[2] *Ibid.*, November 5, 1778

[3] " Hope addressing Peace, Art and Labour" (see receipt facing
p. 204.)

there seem to be none left now. It is possible the ship was wrecked and the whole consignment was lost, yet the fact that there is one remaining suggests that others may also be hidden away. Any of the 199 would be a " find." " I shall send you a few of " the medals as soon as I get a second parcel, having " despatched all the first to London for fear the ship " should sail without them." [1]

There are some interesting passages in the letters from Governor Phillips, which are now preserved in the Mitchell Library at Sydney, New South Wales, which refer to the consignments of clay sent to Wedgwood and the receipt of medallions and other pieces that were made from it. In a letter dated November 16, 1788, referring to some casks which were sent to Wedgwood care of Sir J. Banks we have : " N° 1. " contains the white Clay with wch the natives mark " themselves, it is found in great plenty a few feet " below the surface & by what I have observed two " or three feet in thickness, under the Strata of this " Clay there generally is rock, but we have only " open'd three or four places, the people use it to " cover their Houses. I should not think it worth " sending, but that you mention'd it in your Voyage, " & l'Abbe Mongey, a very sensible man, & I believe " a good naturalist, told me that it would make good " China. When at Broken Bay I saw on a small " Island a few feet below the sand on the beach a " white Clay that was much finer than any we have " here." [2]

---

[1] Wedgwood to Darwin, November 1789.
[2] Letter from Governor Phillips to Sir Joseph Banks.

Reference to more clay being sent out, and proof that one consignment at least of medallions reached there, appears in the following extract : " I have " never heard of the Convict Potter coming out, " two small Casks of Clay were to have been sent " by the Neptune, but I shall send them with some " others by the Gorgon. The Cup & Medallions " with the Vases were received & for which as well " as all your friendly attentions many thanks." [1]

Still another letter refers to the cup and medallions, and also further consignments of clay : " Wedgwood " has showed the World that our Welch Clay is capable " of receiving an Elegant impression & I return thanks " for the Cup & Medallions. There is some Clay by " the Gorgon for Wedgwood, I think that is the least " we can do for him." [2]

Another design of great historical interest was made both in cameo and intaglio form and widely distributed, some gratuitously and some by sale. " The Slave," a very perfect piece of modelling, was done by Hackwood, and illustrates very fully how he excelled in this particular class of work, enabling us to appreciate Wedgwood's remark, " These things he does admirably," which we feel would have been made as freely and unstintingly with regard to his original work ten years later as it was said of his repairing and adapting of these things before.

This design was made for, and approved by, the Committee of the Society for the Abolition of Slavery, and adopted by them as a seal. It also formed the frontispiece to their pamphlets.

[1] Letter from Governor Phillips to Sir Joseph Banks.   [2] Ibid.

A series of cameos, all of the Apotheosis type of design, and having in some form a reference to the German Empire, has caused much inquiry, as specimens are found in many collections. One invoice sent to Byerley (nephew of Wedgwood and partner in the firm after January 1, 1790) at Frankfurt a/M. shows a consignment of 186 of these, all with a fine blue ground and thus described :—

> " 30 Upr^t oval cameos,   Fame inscribing Vase to memory of Elizabeth.   1.7/8".

> " 22 Upr^t oval Bent   do.   do.   1.1/8"

> " 23 Upr^t oval Cameos.   Leopold the Lawgiver support^d by Wisdom & Benevolence.   1.7/8".

> " 57   Do.   do.   do.   nearly 1.3/8".

> " 19 round Cameos.   The Genius of the Empire holding the Bust of Leopold while a priestess is officiating at an altar.   full 2.1/8".

> " 17 r^d Cameos.   Germany, in the Character of Minerva present^g Leopold with a Civic band as a reward for his code of Laws.   full 2.1/8".

> " 7 r^d Cameos.   Mars present^g a Crown to the Genius of Germany, to be placed upon the bust of Leopold which stands on an Altar.   full 2.1/8".

> " 4 r^d Cameos.   Turkey & Russia & the two belligerant powers, consulting upon peace, & Germany the mediator between them.   full 2.1/8".

> " 7 Upr^t oval Cameos.   Coronation of Leopold. full 2"."

Leopold II, Emperor of Germany, succeeded his brother in February 1790, and the last item in the invoice had been prepared in anticipation of the coronation taking place in that year. The letter accompanying this invoice has the following query : " One of our papers gives us reason to suppose that " there will not be any coronation at Frankfurt this " year. What do you think of this matter ? " [1]

The uses to which cameos were applied are almost too numerous to mention ; one comes across them continually in fresh settings, in necklaces, chatelaines, bracelets, rings, watch keys, scarf pins, hat pins, buttons, and brooches, and other kinds of jewellery. Some were introduced into the hilts of dress swords, and many snuffboxes and dressing-table requisites, patch boxes and the like, were adorned with them. (See illus. facing p. 189.)

Some of the finest were made for the outside cases of the old verge watches, and these being thinner and more fragile, have not survived to the same extent. These were about $1\frac{1}{2}$ inches diameter, convex and concave as the shape of the watchcase, and were only mounted by the bezel. The subjects are classical groups, very delicately modelled in low relief, giving full value to the translucency of the white jasper body upon the coloured background.

The collection of portrait medallions of Wedgwood has always called forth the greatest praise ; it was especially worthy of it in the section of his " Illustrious Moderns " which gave opportunity for utilising the work of any of the artists and sculptors of his day whom he sought out for the purpose. This section, which comprises some of the best examples of a form of miniature sculpture which has almost ceased to be

[1] Wedgwood to Byerley, September 19, 1790.

1.

2.

1. PORTRAIT MEDALLION, JASPER, "THE QUEEN OF PORTUGAL."
2. PORTRAIT MEDALLION, JASPER, IN ORMOLU GILT FRAME, "THE
EMPEROR OF GERMANY."

3.

4.

3. PORTRAIT MEDALLION, JASPER, "WASHINGTON."
4. PORTRAIT MEDALLION, JASPER, "FRANKLIN."

(Etruria Museum.)

[To face page 186.

1.   2.

1. PORTRAIT MEDALLION, JASPER, "THE REV. WILLIAM WILLETT."
2. PORTRAIT MEDALLION, JASPER, "THOMAS BYERLEY."

3.   4.

3. PORTRAIT MEDALLION, JASPER, "KEMBLE."
4. PORTRAIT MEDALLION, JASPER, "MRS. EDGEWORTH."

(Etruria Museum.)

[To face page 187.

nowadays, has become the one chosen by some to form a collection, and is perhaps the most original and unique of all Wedgwood's work.

In the classical set we have the kings and illustrious persons of Asia, Egypt, and Greece, from the time of the Trojan War to the settling of the Roman Empire in Constantinople, including queens, statesmen, philosophers, orators and poets, a set of twelve Cæsars in four sizes, and their empresses in one size. These when found marked with the Wedgwood & Bentley stamp are worth adding to any collection. A sequel set of fifty-two Emperors, from Nerva to Constantine the Great, the Popes, the Kings and Queens of England, and the Kings of France, were made with and without frames in basaltes.

The heads of illustrious moderns included those from Chaucer (A.D. 1400) to the present time, which may be a movable date and only refer to those which were modelled during Wedgwood's lifetime, or may be extended to cover the work of those sculptors who supplied models afterwards, among which must be included the four admirals, Nelson, Duncan, Vincent, and Howe, attributed to Devære, although no proof is obtainable. These came to Etruria after 1795. It is not likely, however, that much was done in this branch during the last few years of the eighteenth, and early ones of the nineteenth century.

The number appearing in the 1779 catalogue was 177, and this had increased to 227 in the catalogue of 1788. Modern portraiture in medallion and cameo form seems to have started about 1774, one of the first being that of Lady Charlotte Finch, referred to

in connection with two gentlemen's heads that were
sent for making, but were not suitable for the purpose
as compared with the lady's already made. Those of
Mrs. Montague and Mrs. Barbault were modelled in
1775.

That definite progress had been made and development anticipated during this year is shown in the
following extract from a letter written in August :
" only I wish you to see Mr. Flaxman before you
" leave London, & if you could prevail upon him to
" finish Mr Banks & Dr Solander they would be an
" acquisition to us, & as we shall now make with
" tolerable certainty any moderate sized Bassreliefs
" of the composition sent you last in a Conquer'd
" Province & companion, I submit it to you whether
" we should not have some of the finest things that
" can be modeled, and Originals which have not been
" hackney'd in Wax & Plaister for a century past,
" & if you think we should, would it not be saving
" time to set Mr. Flaxman upon some business before
" you leave him." [1]

In the January of the next year " several pairs of
" Banks & Solanders, & we are making more," are
mentioned as having been sent to London with other
heads wanted. About this time much attention was
paid to these portraits, for a letter of February 1776
gives a list showing what had been modelled, and
includes forty-eight Greek heads and seventy-four
illustrious moderns, eleven of them only noted as
having been taken from medals.

Constant care was given to the perfecting of these

[1] Wedgwood to Bentley, August 1775.

COLLECTION OF STEEL MOUNTED JASPER CAMEOS.

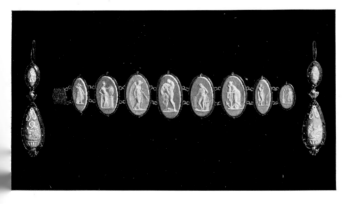

JASPER CAMEOS MOUNTED AS TWO EARRINGS AND A BRACELET.
(Etruria Museum.)

[To face page 188.

I.   2.   3.   4.   5.

I. CAMEO, JASPER, MOUNTED IN A CASE.
2. DOUBLE INTAGLIO, BASALTES, MOUNTED AS A WATCH KEY.
3. CAMEO, JASPER, MOUNTED IN THE LID OF A PATCH BOX.
4. CAMEO, JASPER, MOUNTED AS WATCH CASE.
5. CAMEO, JASPER, MOUNTED IN SCENT BOTTLE.

6.

6. CAMEO, JASPER, SHOWING THE REVERSE SIDE OF NO. I.

(British Museum.)

[To face page 189.

portraits ; what each demanded it received : " We send
" you a few of our new Edition of the K & Q I wish
" they were better, You'l see how the blue has stained
" her Majesty, We must make those parts thicker ;
" but that will take more time, new moulds &c, &
" we have clay, everlasting, moulds already. An
" hundred of these little teizeing accidents are daily
" springing up in our finest works, like Tares amongst
" Wheat, & the finer the Wheat the more Tares spring
" up amongst it, which keeps one in a continual fret." [1]

An appreciation of Hackwood's success in original
portraiture is given in the postscript : " I send you
" the head of Mr. Willet [2] as a specimen of Hack-
" wood's Portrait Modelling. A stronger likeness can
" scarcely be conciev'd." [3] A date can also be given
to the large size heads of the Empress of Russia
and Sir Isaac Newton and Rousseau. " The Empress
" of Russia is nearly finished to moulding. It is not
" such a fine Head as the one we had before, but
" considerably larger. Sr Isaac Newton, & Rousseau
" are in hand, but they are not the work of a day." [4]
Dr. Franklin and Linnæus are also mentioned as
being made at this time.

" Old Bourne," the bricklayer at Etruria, is one of
Hackwood's models, and his fine old head has become
quite famous in the collections of medallions. Wedgwood said of it : " Old Bournes is the man himself
" with every wrinkle, crink and cranny in the whole
" visage." This was modelled in 1778.

[1] Wedgwood to Bentley, July 5, 1776.
[2] See illus. facing p. 187.
[3] Wedgwood to Bentley, July 5, 1779.
[4] *Ibid.*, December 15, 1776.

Hackwood had also been set to work upon many portrait models, but they are difficult to identify, as Wedgwood had an objection to the artist putting his name upon any work. " Our new Shakespeare & "Garrick . . . you will see by looking under the shoulder " of each that these heads are modeled by W^m hack-"wood, but I shall prevent his exposing himself " again now I have found out. I am not certain " that he will not be offended if he is refus'd the " liberty of putting his name to the models which " he makes quite new, & I shall be glad to have your " opinion upon the subject. Mine is against any " name being upon our articles besides W & B, & " if you concur with me I will manage the matter " with him as well as I can." [1]

When Admiral Keppel was the man of the hour in 1779, Byerley was travelling from town to town on business and reported that the Admiral's head, if he had it, would sell in thousands. Wedgwood wrote to Bentley in London bemoaning the fact, in his characteristic way, that they had not been cute enough to foresee it. " Oh Keppel, Keppel, Why " will not you send me a Keppel. I am perswaded " if we had had our wits about us as we ought to " have had 2 or 3 months since we might have sold " £1,000 worth of this gentleman's heads in various " ways, & I am perswaded it would still be worth " while to disperse them every way in our power. " But we must first have possession before we dispose " of him." [2] No time was lost, for the same month

[1] Wedgwood to Bentley, December 22, 1777.
[2] *Ibid.*, March 1, 1779.

reveals the making of a portrait from a print, and a gentleman who was visiting the works, seeing it lying upon the table without any name to it or any intimation as to who it was, said, " So I see you have the Admiral, and it is a good likeness of him." [1]

This was in a few days sent to London, and the question was asked as to the probability of the sale of a few thousands in pictures, rings, seals, lockets, etc. Before a month had passed Keppel was finished " of the large size, The $2\frac{1}{2}$ inch & for rings and seals. " Of the latter we have orders from Birm[m] &c for 20 " doz." [2]

This record gives some idea of the way in which these matters were attacked and successfully despatched, and leaves us reflecting upon the limited facilities and slow communication that existed, thus emphasising that determination to overcome all obstacles which gave us the rich result that we have.

A very large size medallion was modelled of Keppel ; this mould is still in the mould chamber at Etruria ; it measures 18 inches from the top of the head to the bottom of the bust, which would when fired contract to about 15 inches. It is most probable that none of these were made, as the mould shows no sign of having been used. This remark applies also to a similar medallion, the same size, of Bentley, the mould of which was destroyed many years since. These were the only two extra large size portraits of which models were made. In the letter dated March 8, 1779, is a distinct statement : " We have

[1] Wedgwood to Bentley, March 15, 1779.
[2] Wedgwood to Byerley, May 20, 1779.

" under hand of Admiral Keppel, a bust of the size
" of Geo. the 2nd " ; but this seems to be one thing
that was never completed.

Dr. Priestley and Sir Isaac Newton, forming a pair,
are referred to first in 1779, when the model of the
former was sent to Etruria : " D^r. Priestley is arriv^d
" & we are with great reverance taking off his pres-
" byterian parsons wig & preparing a Sr I. Newton
" as a companion to him." [1]   A model of Flaxman's
head came at the same time, and Sir Wm. Hamilton's
was also being modelled ; these, with another Franklin,
were sent for comment and approval to London in
May.

This year was a very busy one, and important
additions were made to the portrait gallery of illustrious moderns. Many of the smaller heads were
modelled to a larger size : " We have bosted him
" out (S^r W^m) the size of Mr Banks, & I think a suit
" of eminent moderns, naturalists, amateurs &c should
" be made of the same size, & stile, & so form a con-
" stellation, as it were, to attract the notice of the
" great, & illuminate every palace in Europe." [2]

The models in this section as now represented upon
the works and in the Museum at Etruria in the form
of waxes, shell moulds and block moulds, number
about four hundred, of which about one-fifth cannot
be identified, but the style of treatment in relief and
modelling places them without any doubt in the same
series as those which belong to the period mentioned
above.

[1] Wedgwood to Byerley, March 24, 1779.
[2] Wedgwood to Bentley, September 2, 1779.

VIII

SCULPTORS
ARTISTS
CRAFTSMEN

CHAPTER VIII

SCULPTORS, ARTISTS, CRAFTSMEN

THE faculty of utilising material of every type and
form was developed to the full in Wedgwood and
redounds to his credit, for he missed no opportunity
of acquiring any assistance that would help him to
reach the goal of his ambitions, and with true business
acuteness he was ever on the look-out for talent that

could be made adaptable to his need. At the commencement of his career as a master potter this need was very great, for besides the ordinary workmen of the potteries there was no artist at hand ; books and examples of fine work in any craft were non-existent, except such as were out of sight in the houses of the gentry of the neighbourhood, and therefore he had to import them from outside and form for himself the collection of those things which would tend to elevate and train the taste of those whom he had picked out as being capable of receiving such special instruction. He made his own school of art and studio where these physical and mental abilities were carefully developed and trained.

Much has been written and said about the help he obtained from outside, and that he used it as fully as possible cannot be gainsaid, but too great a stress must not be laid upon it. He sought and obtained models from any likely source, and a fair amount of original work came from some of the most prominent artists of the day, but a point that has not been emphasised before is that praise should be given to the artists who worked silently unknown, the modellers at Etruria, who after all had the final veto on all work that came from outside, and who made and finished for the practical potter every model that was put into their hands for reproduction.

When looking upon the matter from this side, we must acknowledge how technical a thing is pottery, how little those who have not been brought up in the atmosphere of a " pot-bank " know about the art and mystery of it, so that it can easily be understood how little even the best artist outside would know about the difficulties and details required to supply a good model.

Among the names of those associated with Wedgwood, that of John Flaxman, afterwards R.A., stands at the head, and quite rightly should it take that place, but in the course of time it has come to be assumed that everything worthy of notice must be Flaxman's, and much has been assigned to him that belongs to others.

To look at the evidence as we have it untainted, in Wedgwood's own letters to Bentley, will at any rate place the facts in order, and will not take away any of the praise due to him who after Wedgwood's death became a great academician, nor remove the credit from any of the able craftsmen who alone made his work possible in Wedgwood Ware.

Wedgwood gave unstinted praise to the original work of William Hackwood, and we cannot think that such a keen critic would have done so had not this been amply justified, which can be verified by the known specimens of Hackwood's work. We find references to failures in the work of others which have to be made good by Hackwood.

The father of John Flaxman was also John Flaxman, and care must be exercised in sifting out the evidence that we have. The father was a maker of plaster models, from the antique, and supplied a great many models of antique works of art, etc., that would be useful to Wedgwood. Many invoices for these goods exist with the signature showing receipt of payment, but in some cases this has been confused with the son's signature, and thus many plaster casts supplied have been taken to be from original work by the son and put down to his credit. As actual proof is wanting, definite pieces cannot be cited, but it is probable that some of the early pieces of basaltes assigned to Flaxman are in reality adapted from models in plaster taken from the antique and supplied by Flaxman senior. This is apparent from the letter quoted earlier in reference to busts, where he says : " This is from the " Academy taken from an Original—than to say, we " had it from Flaxman." [1]   The first mention of young Flaxman is during this same year, when a Mr. Freeman visited the works.   He was a man of taste and had travelled a great deal—" but says as our materials " are so fine, & we execute so well, we sho^d, to be " complete, spare no expence in having the finest things " abroad model^d for us, . . . he is a great admirer " of young Flaxman & had advis'^{d} his Father to " send him to Rome, which he has promis'^{d} to do. " Mr Freeman says he knows young Flaxman is a " Coxcomb, but does not think him a bit the worse " for it, or less likely to be a great Artist." [2]

The next reference to him comes four years later : " I am glad you have met with a Modeler, & that " Flaxman is so valuable an Artist.—It is but a few " years since he was a most supreme Coxcomb, but " a little more experience may have cured him of " that foible." [3]

During this year the idea of utilising the work of

[1] Wedgwood to Bentley, February 16, 1771.

[2] *Ibid.*, September 7, 1771.

[3] *Ibid.*, January 14, 1775.

young Flaxman must have been seriously considered, for Sir Thos. Broughton desires to have the portraits of his two boys modelled, to put into a pair of bracelets as jasper cameos to present to his Lady, and Wedgwood asks what the expense would be, adding : " I suppose " Mr Flaxman will be more moderate than Mr Smith." [1] In the same month the definite suggestion comes, which has the savour of a first trial about it : " Suppose " you were to employ Mr Flaxman to model some " figures — They would do for Tablets, Vases, inlaying, " &c." [2] The first mention of the receipt of a model comes a year after, with the comment upon it, " The " model is too small to go along with Cupid shav^g his " Bow &c.—I will endeavour to ascertain the size we " should have the models & give you the dimensions " along with this by the coach," [3] which also seems to refer to a first model, as any point like this would only be raised about the early work sent ; the technical point in this case referring to the contraction which took place in firing the necessary clay moulds before the working moulds were ready for making the figures for applying to the ware.

Flaxman was engaged upon more basreliefs, for the next letter sends correct sizes for him to work to, and a fortnight later, to avoid duplication in London, there is sent a list of subjects that are being modelled at the works, in which is specially mentioned a " Medea "— " The same you have sent us by the last Coach, only " higher relief. Mr Flaxman's is too flat in several

[1] Wedgwood to Bentley, July 8, 1775.
[2] Ibid., July 20, 1775.
[3] Ibid., June 19, 1776.

" parts to be made in colour'^d grounds, & we can
" sooner finish our own than raise his model. I am
" aware of the necessity a Modeler will plead for
" making some parts so flat, in order to keep those
" parts back, & to give a proper relief to the whole.
" But you will soon see, by turning to our blue
" & white Jaspers, that we cannot admit of such
" delicate parts, & must be content with such effects
" in our Figures as can be produc'^d without
" them." [1]

Here is the part in which the artist on the works
excelled, and in which he succeeded, for the great mass
of figure work that has emanated from Etruria has
satisfied all, and this is a case where even Flaxman's
work had to be remodelled.

The Muses were certainly modelled by Flaxman.
" I am sorry the Muse is so small —— Have you
" examin'^d the finishing of this model ? It will cost us
" half a guinea to make it equal in that respect to the
" other statues." [2] This in all probability refers to the
first " Muse " that was modelled, and that this defect
was remedied and the work proceeded with appears
from the letter two months later, which acknowledges
the possession of four of the set and an urgent request
for the rest. " You may permit Mr Flaxman to
" proceed with the Muses of the size he had begun,
" they will be very usefull to us, & I would give half
" the price of modelling extra to be in possession of
" them now, so be so good to expedite him all you
" can. We have Apollo, Melpomena, Thalia & Terpsi-

---

[1] Wedgwood to Bentley, July 9, 1776.
[2] *Ibid.*, May 15, 1777.

" chore, so that we only want 6 more to complete our
" suite." [1]

The desire to hurry forward this set accounts for
the action which is recorded in a letter sent only two
days after, the paragraph referring to it being :
" Having laid all our bassrelief Goddesses & ladies upon
" their backs on a board before me in order to contem-
" plate their beauties, & to increase their number, I
" instantly perciev'd that the six Muses we want might
" be produc'd from this lovely group at half the trouble
" and expence they will be procured from Flaxman,
" & much better figures.—I hope you may not have
" order'd them to be model'd as I desir'd you would,
" but if you have, so be it,—it is only so much loss.
" If he has not begun upon them you might give him
" as good an order in a Tablet, & all would be right
" again." [2] There is little doubt, however, that the
order had been given and the whole set modelled, and
supplied by Flaxman. (See illus. facing p. 168.)

The " Dancing Hours," another well-known set of
figures which have formed the subject of many tablets
and vases, were originally supplied by Flaxman, but
this is not the set which later became so famous, and
have been generally associated with his name. The
figures which appear on the friezes of vases, and form
the subjects of placques (from a single figure to six or
even more) are not those which were supplied by
Flaxman. Presumably the original set of block moulds
of Flaxman's " Dancing Hours " were destroyed, as
no trace of them remains. The frieze of twelve figures

---

[1] Wedgwood to Bentley, October 27, 1777.
[2] *Ibid.*, October 29, 1777.

existing now were modelled by Hackwood in 1802, and these have been erroneously assigned to Flaxman.

The original figures by Flaxman are shown on two placques which are now in the Museum at Etruria. An illustration of one of them is given. (See illus. facing p. 168.) Upon examination the difference in the draping of the figures will be very noticeable, the originals being faithful reductions of the figures in the frieze from which they were taken, while Hackwood's version was produced in accordance with the feeling which he had acquired from Wedgwood when he was prompted to write about similar figures to Bentley fifteen years before. The relief of the modelling, freedom and grace of pose, disposition of the drapery, and general chaste interpretation, have certainly removed the somewhat Bacchanalian suggestion of the original set. (See illus. facing p. 205.)

There is no wish to detract from the beautiful work which Flaxman supplied, more especially in later years, but only a desire to place Hackwood in his rightful position, as the artist who was responsible for the standard and quality of the work. He prepared the models, renovating and finishing the work that was sent in from outside ; he overlooked the moulds and superintended the making of the first pieces, touching them up and passing them on to the final stage of firing, only when they satisfied both himself and his master.

There is a note of great satisfaction in the sentence, " We have a very perfect one [1] from Mr. Flaxman's " model, & have several more in hand of different " subjects. You shall have a most glorious assort-

[1] Referring to a tablet.

" ment for the opening of the next season, of Tablets,
" frises & blocks to go together in the composition of
" a chimney piece." [1]

Flaxman went to Rome in 1787, but still continued
his connection with Wedgwood, who had occasion to
write him a rather lengthy letter containing good
wishes, a suggestion of reproof for only having received
one letter from him, acknowledging at the same time
that he knew he went to Rome for study, and not to
keep up a correspondence with his friends in England.
He makes complaint as to the state in which the last
relief models came to hand, because of imperfect
packing, and adds some interesting details about
modelling that Devære was doing for him, and the
kind attention that Flaxman was giving to the choice
of subjects for him to model.

There is very little actual record of the work which
can be definitely traced to Flaxman, but the portrait
medallions given below are his, the six names added
after are probably his also.

Of the tablets it is more difficult to judge. The
" Mercury joining the hands of France and England,"
and " Peace preventing Mars from bursting the Gates
of Janus," are certainly his, and also the three subjects,
" The Apotheosis of Homer," " The Apotheosis of
Virgil," and " Hercules in the Garden of the Hesperides," but the remainder of those generally assigned to
him must be looked upon as more or less direct copies
from the antique, supplied to the works and adapted
and finished by other hands for the purposes they
were required.

[1] Wedgwood to Bentley, August 9, 1778.

The models which can be identified as Flaxman's are :—

Portraits :

The Earl of Chatham (2 models).
Capt. James Cook. (See illus. facing p. 179.)
Hon. Warren Hastings.
Hon. C. Jenkinson.
Sir Frederic W. Herschel.
Sir Joseph Banks.
Dr. Solander.
Sir Joshua Reynolds.
John Flaxman (2 models).
Dr. Buchan.
Dr. Fothergill.
Mr. Meerman.
Lady Banks.
Mrs. Edgeworth.   (See illus. facing p. 187.)
Mrs. Meerman.

Those assigned to him, but without actual proof, are:

Mrs. Siddons.
Michael A. de Ruyter.
Jacob Cats.
Dr. Samuel Johnson.
Goethe (2 models).
The Duchess of Devonshire.

One set of the Muses—the medium size—is also his, but " The Choice of Hercules," for which he has so universally received the credit, appears in the catalogue of 1774, before Flaxman had any connection with Wedgwood.

William Hackwood was engaged by Wedgwood in

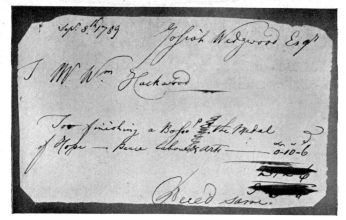

1.

2.

3.

4.

(Etruria Museum.)

[To face page 204.

1. RAISED BLOCK MOULD OF A FERN LEAF, BY HACKWOOD, MADE IN HIS 72ND YEAR.
2 & 3. BACK AND FRONT OF A PLASTER BLOCK MOULD OF HACKWOOD'S DANCING FIGURES.
4 & 5. INTAGLIO BLOCK MOULDS USED FOR MAKING SEALS.
6, 7, & 8. TYPE TRIALS SHOWING OVEN REFERENCE MARKS.

1769 (this was the ingenious boy referred to in the letter written to Bentley [1] on September 20, 1769) and continued to work at Etruria until 1832. During this period he seems to have been the most trusted and capable, able to deal with all the finishing of figures, busts, medallions, cameos and seals ; his technique and skill in the two last mentioned being perfectly marvellous. In 1770 we first hear of him in the position which generally falls to the lot of a modeller upon a " works," not as a specialist, but a good all-round man, capable of putting his hand to any class of work that requires the touch of the artist. " We shall " make some flowerpots upon the Idea you give me in " this letter when we can model them, but Hackwood " has been 3 weeks upon one of the flower baskets & " is not ingaged in finishing bassreliefs." [2] He very soon showed his desire for, and tried his hand at, original work, for a year afterwards, when the question of modelling the portraits of the King and Queen is raised, Wedgwood writes : " we have made a sort of beginning " in that way here, for Hackwood has been three times " at Crew, by Mrs Crews particular desire to model " the head of her son & heir. I told her he was quite " a novice in Portrait modelling, but she wo^{d} have him " try his hand, & I could not refuse her. What he " will make of it I do not know." [3] Judging by the portraits which he afterwards modelled and the praise that he received from Wedgwood, we may safely say that this was a most fortunate and successful digression, as the portraits of George III and Queen Charlotte

[1] See p. 213.   [2] Wedgwood to Bentley, August 20, 1770.
[3] *Ibid.*, September 7, 1771.

that he made, and which are among the few that he
signed, will prove.

His painstaking ability and capacity for minute work
is acknowledged in a letter partly obliterated by time,
but quite clear in its reference to the preparing of fine
seals : " Hackwood is ——ing " (probably making or
modelling) " Stampes from many of the best small
" heads—his work at these things is excellent, and
" tho' it takes time I hope it will answer well, as the
" value of these fine things can only be Preserved by
" great care." [1]   It was his work that was commented
upon when Bentley was told that the busts would be
found to be much finer and better finished than the
plaster ones, and upon each one he put a whole week's
work in restoring it to its original state.   This can be
fully appreciated when we examine any of the black
basaltes busts.   And yet caution is needed ; the same
breath blows hot and cold : a doubt arises as to the
finishing of some important figures, " will Hackwood
be capable," followed by the remark in the same
sentence that he would improve them : " I must send
" you a few of the new model'd figures as they are,
" for Hackwood, if he is capable of giving character to
" their faces, & improving the draperies, wch I have some
" doubt of, though I am perswaded he would mend
" them considerably, he has no time for it at present.—
" The Busts will employ him for a year or two." [2]

No greater praise can be given to Hackwood than
Wedgwood himself accords four years later when he
clearly states that he is taking under review all his

---

[1] Wedgwood to Bentley, February 1773.
[2] *Ibid.*, September 11, 1774.

tablets and improving them by the aid of Hackwood's work. If a careful study of the various subjects in these tablets is made, it will be noticed how much is due to this very "improving" review that was made. The finish and perfection of detail that are so much admired resulted from this review, and have as much to do with the appreciation given to these old pieces as the subject or origin of the model, and these qualities we claim for Hackwood. "Some of the tablets lately " sent are finish'd very high by Hackwood at a " considerable expence. I may perhaps name them " to you in a P.S. but if I should not you will easily " percieve the difference in the hair, faces, fingers, &c, " & more palpably by all the parts capable of it being " under cut which gives them the appearance, & nearly " the reality of models. We propose for the future, " in order to give these fine things every perfection in " our power, & ourselves a character, with posterity " at least, to remodel them all the same way, which " step I flatter myself will meet with your approba- " tion." [1] This was followed by a letter four days later which gives more information upon this intention, and shows how the frieze of the Muses after this date became an improved edition, which was sent along for comparison with a frieze of the same from the first moulds : " We shall make the frises of the muses finer for the " time to come. That is Hackwood will repair—restore " & undercut them, & I mention this circumstance " now that you may take advantage of this improve- " ment for M^{rs} M^s [2] fine house if you think proper.

[1] Wedgwood to Bentley, November 4, 1778.
[2] Probably Mrs. Montague.

" It will be 5 or 6 weeks before you have any of these
" improv'd ones, & those you have are very fine, so do
" what you please with them.   You will see a specimen
" of the Muses improv'd in a tablet, or picture 25 in^s
" by 8 containing the whole nine, & sent by the waggon
" to-day along with an Homer & Hesiod tablet, & a
" frise of the Muses, not improv'd." [1]

Hackwood's work continued until 1832, and the
models that can be definitely traced to him are :—

Portraits :

    George III (3 models).   (See illus. facing p. 179.)

    Queen Charlotte (2 models). (See illus. facing p. 179.)

    Louis XVI.

    Rev. William Willet.   (See illus. facing p. 187.)

    Shakespeare (2 models).   (See illus. facing p. 179.)

    David Garrick.

    Josiah Wedgwood.

    Edward Bourne (the Etruscan bricklayer).

    Admiral Keppel.

Medallions :

    Indian Bacchus.

    Roman Matron.

    Sophonisba ⎤

    Hercules   ⎟

    Piping Faun ⎬ Figures.

    Plenty   ⎟

    Medea   ⎦

    Antony.   Cleopatra.

Tablets :

    " The Birth of Bacchus."   (See illus. facing p. 168.)

    " The Triumph of Bacchus."

        [1] Wedgwood to Bentley, November 8, 1778.

The medallion " Hope addressing Peace, Art and Labour," always attributed to Webber, was, as we see it complete, Hackwood's work—the exquisite finish was his, even if the design was another's ; in proof of which see the receipt for the payment. (See illus. facing p. 204.)

Again, it has been universally said that Webber modelled the figures for the Portland Vase, but this is not likely or even possible, for the vase only came to Etruria in 1786. The frieze of figures was modelled three times before it satisfied Wedgwood, which task could not have been completed in twelve months, and in 1787 Webber was in Rome with John Wedgwood ; therefore, as Hackwood was the only modeller on the Etruria Works, it is only fair to put this work also to his credit.

Webber was one of the modellers who worked at Etruria. He was a most capable man, recommended by Sir Wm. Chambers and Sir Joshua Reynolds, and was esteemed the first in his profession in England. He had the advantage of a more complete training in Art generally than any others who were engaged, and he held the position of Manager in the studios. Two models that can be assigned to him are the two branched candelabra " Diana " and " Minerva." The beautiful medallion commemorating the forming of the new colony of New South Wales, the subject of which was " Hope addressing Peace, Art and Labour," and which inspired Erasmus Darwin to poetry in his " Botanic Garden," has always been associated with his name, but, as already pointed out, this is highly improbable. His opinion and advice were greatly appreciated by Wedgwood, who consulted him upon the question of the proposed visit of his son Tom to Rome. He also accompanied young John Wedgwood on a tour in Wales and was on the Continent one season with him. He worked at Etruria from 1782 till 1794.

Tebo was a modeller about whom much has been said, chiefly because some writer jumped to the conclusion that the letters T.B.O. stamped on certain pieces of ware found were the signature of the artist, whereas in reality they were stamped upon a trial to indicate permanently the position it had occupied in the oven (Top Biscuit Oven) for future reference. Wedgwood's estimate of him and his work was not very great, and he never minced matters with regard to either in his correspondence with Bentley. The first reference is : " Mr Tebo, our new Modeler, did " not return here for some days after me, & I am glad " he did not for he would have made a shocking Ugly " thing of the Lamp if he had been left to himself. " But he has sprain'd his Arm, & has done very little " work at present." [1] Later in the month we hear he is modelling two lamps but goes on very slowly, and a very doubtful compliment is paid to him when Wedgwood writes : " Mr Tebo may be a usefull hand for " large things but he cannot finish anything small." [2]

He was employed in repairing figures and heads, and the verdict was that he did these large things very well, but no reliance could be placed upon him, for he is not allowed to do any original work : " I think we can " manage to model them, & Mr Tebo has nothing else " to do. He is not equal to a Figure, but I can make

---

[1] Wedgwood to Bentley, November 5, 1774.
[2] *Ibid.*, January 1, 1775.

" him bost out & others finish these Heads." [1] In
October of the same year he seems to have run the full
length of his tether : " Mr Tebo leaves us the 11th of
" this Month, and not before he has done us very con-
" siderable mischief, for our Modelers do less by one half
" than they did before, charging double prices for their
" work, & when talk'd to about it have their reply
" ready ' that it is cheaper than Mr Tebo's, & is finished,
" which his work never is.' " [2] He went to Dublin,
where he started to model portraits, and applied to
Etruria asking what they would charge to make his
portraits in their fine Jasper body. Wedgwood's
comment to Bentley is : " I am afraid his Models will
" do our white Jasper no credit, but I shall write to
" Mr Brock [3] that he is not to be consider'd as our
" Modeler, & that we shall answer only for the exact-
" ness of the copies from the original they may send us,
" and for the goodness of the material." [4] This will
be sufficient to show that there is no great credit due
to Tebo in connection with his work at Etruria.

The present chapter is devoted, as will be readily
seen, to giving credit where it is due. So much has
been written about one or two, and so little about
the large staff of really clever men who assisted in the
production of what is considered, and rightly so, the
pioneer work in connection with the artistic side at
least, and largely the technical ; one also, of English
pottery. Although the names may be almost unknown

---

[1] Wedgwood to Bentley, July 3, 1775.
[2] *Ibid.*, October 28, 1775.
[3] Wedgwood's agent in Dublin.
[4] Wedgwood to Bentley, July 6, 1776.

now, they are recorded, and it is not idle fancy to try
to visualise them through their work, for whatever
the copy or pattern or suggestion put into their hands,
the translation of it into pottery must be acknowledged
as original work. In the earlier days the modellers
and artists were as important and essential as at any
subsequent time, so that some slight gleaning of facts
will add to the interest of those productions. Though
the information be scanty, it will detach certain things
from the mass, if they can be definitely attributed to
a certain man at a known period.

Boot was one of the early modellers, and we are told
that he modelled " some sad figures, but he will never-
" theless be made a usefull hand," [1] which was proved
very soon afterwards, as he was sent to Etruria from
the works at Burslem to start upon terra-cotta
figures, a " Sphynx, Lyon & Triton " to begin with,
and to bring up hands to figure making, but seems
afterwards to have become a good figure maker himself, and was responsible for many sphinxes, tritons,
and figures for the covers of vases.

Denby was another whose position was an important
one in preserving the standard of work which the
Master had set up, and to him we owe much when our
eye rests satisfied upon the shape and outline of a
vase. Wedgwood tells Bentley he intends to go and
live at Etruria—this was before his house was finished—
as it was not sufficient to spend an hour or two there in
a morning, " & take Mr Denby with me . . . he will
" be very usefull to me & help to keep them in ord^r
" with respect to forms which I am convinc'd with you

[1] Wedgwood to Bentley, September 9, 1769.

" is the principal part." [1] An ingenious boy [2] was
hired to assist Denby at Etruria, and to model as
well. " I have hired him for five years, & with
" Denby & him I shall not want any other constant
" modeler at Etruria." [3] Later on we hear that " M[r]
" Denby has Genius & invention as well as taste & will
" be clever." [4] He was adaptable and could turn his
talent to account where it was wanted, for he was sent
to London to Bentley at Chelsea to paint Vases, with
the remark : " he is a better hand than most you'll
" get, is very dilligent & I am sure will get us more
" money & Credit by painting Vases now that we want
" them so much than by modelling of which we are not
" in such immediate want." [5] Finally he migrated to
Derby Works.

Many artists have been named and credited with
supplying models to Wedgwood & Bentley. It is
certain that their work was reproduced at Etruria, but
the task of assigning any particular model to the one
responsible for it is one that probably will never be
completed now. Any record, if kept—which is very
doubtful—has been lost, and most of the models
received from outside at that time were considerably
altered and adapted to suit the material in which they
were afterwards made. But of this group of artists
some definite details remain which will assist a little in
the identification of a few of their works. Wedgwood,
in his catalogues from 1774 onwards, made a special

---

[1] Wedgwood to Bentley, September ?, 1769.
[2] This was Hackwood.
[3] Wedwood to Bentley, September 20, 1769.
[4] *Ibid.*, September 27, ?.
[5] *Ibid.*, May 19, 1770.

notice informing his clients that if they chose to have their portraits modelled in wax or engraven in stones they might have as many durable copies as they pleased in either cameo or intaglio ; and pointed out that this nation possessed several artists who were capable of executing such fine work. Undoubtedly through this invitation much work of this kind was placed in his hands, and from this source came many of the " Illustrious Moderns " series, which were not directly modelled for him.

James Tassie, whose medallions, cameos, and seals are well known, had direct connection with Wedgwood, mainly through Bentley, the first suggestion being made in 1769 with reference to a sacrifice medallion that " Tassie may be a better hand to undertake the " modelling of it," and after the question had been under consideration we get the reference to it again, " I have " no objection to employing Tassie, but the money," [1] as though the price would be too heavy for them in those early days. Whether he supplied any models at this time does not appear, but after he had started making portrait medallions, and was receiving some amount of patronage, the price at which he sold his productions raised the question as to the advisability of selling the jasper ones at the same price, and the confession had to be made that their seal trade had suffered terrible depredations owing to his success in seal making.

Amicable relations, however, existed, for Tassie at one time supplied seventy impressions in sulphur to Wedgwood & Bentley, presumably small heads for seals ;

[1] Wedgwood to Bentley, November 19, 1769.

and as the same portraits and subjects exist in both jasper and Tassie glass enamel, it is reasonable to suppose that these relations remained to the mutual benefit of both manufacturers.

Joachim Smith was a modeller who lived and worked in London, making portraits in wax for the nobility and gentry, and these were copied at first in the biscuit ware and afterwards in the fine white " body " that Wedgwood was introducing at the beginning of 1774. In this case it would be far more correct to say that Wedgwood worked for Smith than to put it the reverse way, as has been the universal plan until now, for it is evident that Smith acquired the customer and made the model, and asked Wedgwood to render it more durable by translating the work into his new material. This is made clear by the extracts from letters now given : " We find it necessary to make stamps for M^r " Smiths Ladies heads, & by that means, with some " fine bodies I have in hand I hope we shall do very " cleverly. But these stamps require some time at " first starting & I must beg of you to bespeak a little " of Mr Smiths patience for us, & his Ladies shall be " the better for it for ever. Please to make my best " comp^ts to Mr Smith & tell him I do not forget him, " but bear him in remembrance every day, and almost " every hour & employ both my head & hands in " his service continually," [1] which is followed by a further message, called forth by some display of impatience on the other side : " I wish Mr Smith wo^d " be quiet a little. I do all I can for him. We had " better take a little time at first than send them im-

[1] Wedgwood to Bentley, July 4, 1774.

" perfect." [1]   This was at the time when he was having
so much trouble with his new Jasper " body," and his
regret to have to disappoint is shown : " I am really
" sorry we cannot gratify the Ladies, & Mr Smith in the
" time they desire, . . . I feel for him, & for our selves,
" but my powers of execution are limited, & I cannot
" work miracles in altering the properties of these
" subtle, & complicated (though native) materials I
" had built my fabrique upon. If I had more time,
" more hands, & more heads I could do something,
" but as it is I must be content to do as well as I can.
" A Man who is in the midst of a course of experim^{ts}
" sho^d not be at home to any thing or any body else
" but that cannot be my case." [2]   However, when the
heads were supplied, some disappointment on the part
of Smith's ladies seems to have existed, for matters
seemed to cool down and negotiations closed, and
Wedgwood was on the look-out for another modeller
who would supply work in a similar way, " as we can
" now certainly make the finest things in the World for
" Portraits." [3]

Mr. Smith had evidently been making use of the
knowledge which he had gained from Etruria in a
manner which displeased Wedgwood, for in a letter
that Wedgwood wrote to Bentley there is no doubt as
to his feelings at that time : " If Mr Smith has been
" dabbling with the Person you apprehend, he may
" have done us a very essential injury, & I wish both
" he & his heads had been at Jericho, before we had had

[1] Wedgwood to Bentley, August 6, 1774.
[2] *Ibid.*, August 30, 1774.
[3] *Ibid.*, December 12, 1774

" anything to do with either, as he may infuse many
" notions into D——s's [1] brain which he has learnt from
" seeing our things, & the free conversations we have
" had with him upon these subjects—Your Burd^{ts} &
" Sm——s & all such flighty, unsolid Genius's are very
" dangerous people to have any sort of connection
" with— They are absolutely mad themselves, & yet,
" in their own conceit, are too wise to be guided by
" anybody else." [2]

Voyez, the modeller, was engaged by Wedgwood
for a term of three years in 1768, but he did not complete one. He was altogether unsatisfactory as an
artist and a man, and was nothing but a thorn in
Wedgwood's side even after he had to part with him
on account of misdemeanour. His modelling for
Etruria was practically of no account.

John Bacon is referred to several times during 1769
as a modeller in George Yard, Holborn, who would be
useful and willing to do work, and is mentioned in
connection with the figures of " Night " and " Day."
He did supply work to Wedgwood, for a receipt exists
among the Mayer MSS. for the sum of £9 15s. for
modelling work done, and a letter refers to a " Bacchus
" & Apollo, by Bacon, Four Seasons, by the same,
" and Andromache & Companion by the same, upon
" a circular ground, they being broad sitting fig^s." [3]

John Charles Lochee was a modeller of some repute
during the end of the eighteenth century and had been
engaged to do some work for Wedgwood in London,

---

[1] Duesbury, of Derby Works.
[2] Wedgwood to Bentley, December 12, 1774.
[3] *Ibid.*, June 5, 1777.

by Bentley, of what sort is not said. " I am glad you
" have given Lochee something to do. We want a
" great deal of modelling, having many things before us,
" within a little of being capital . . . If Lochee is
" capable of anything in that stile you may venture to
" engage him for a time. We could employ him here
" for a year or two in repairing Busts & Figures if we
" durst have him in the Country for Hackwood is of
" the greatest value & consequence in finishing fine
" small work, & of this kind we have & shall have
" enough to employ him constantly." [1] This is the
only reference to him, anything further, however
probable, is conjecture.

A collection which must have been fairly representa-
tive is the set of models that were obtained by a
modeller named Pesez. Bentley acquired these along
with others from various sources, " & the Heads will
" make a very valuable addition to our suite of Modern
" Illustrious Personages. . . . I observe Pesez, the
" Artist to whom we owe most of these Heads, is a
" strong mannerist, & has given a Family likeness to
" them all in the thickness of their lips, & a peculiar,
" bold opening of the Nostril. However he has a free,
" bold touch, Slight & Masterly, & superior to the
" common run of Head-makers. I sorted out his Heads,
" as the production of the same Artist, before I saw
" that he had put his name to them." [2] Here again
we have to be content with this single reference to
him.

This is an interesting note, for in looking over all

[1] Wedgwood to Bentley, September 11, 1774.
[2] Ibid., September 7, 1776.

CARVED WOOD PATTERN OF SOUP TUREEN AND LADLE, BY COWARD.

CARVED WOOD PATTERN OF COMPOTIER AND STAND, BY COWARD.
(Etruria Museum.)

[To face page 218.

1.   2.

I & 2. PAIR OF FLOWERPOTS, JASPER, ENGINE-TURNED DICE WORK
AND RELIEF DECORATION.

3.   4.

3. FLOWERPOT, JASPER.
4. CREAM JUG, JASPER.
(Victoria and Albert Museum)

[To face page 219.

these portrait medallions, it is not easy to place together those which have a " Family likeness " and this goes a long way to prove what capable work the Etruscan modellers, who repaired and finished these models before mould making, were able to put into them, a point perhaps already emphasised sufficiently.

John Coward, the wood carver, was a most useful " find," when in the early days modellers were scarce in the Potteries. It was an example of Wedgwood's resourcefulness that he was able to apply the art of another craft for his own purposes and make good use of it. By this method he was able to get the benefit of training and craftsmanship in design which it would have taken him years to acquire by the slow process of training modellers for himself.

When he had acquired the carved wood model of a vase, or pedestal (made by a craftsman in his own familiar material), he was able to adapt it and make serve the purposes of those about him who understood the capabilities of clay, but who were not then sufficiently competent to make the design. Coward supplied many carved wooden models, and the adaptation of these to pottery is an interesting study, which is made possible by consulting the collection of original wooden models that are still in the Museum at Etruria. As we have noticed in another chapter, Coward was employed for a time in mending vases, so that he can be claimed more definitely as one who worked for Wedgwood, to his instructions, as an employee.

After 1787, when Flaxman went to Rome, a continual flow of subjects—modelled and reduced to suitable sizes from the antique—came to Etruria. Some of these were the work of Flaxman, but in the main they were the work of other artists who were specially engaged there for the purpose, probably working more or less under the direct superintendence of Flaxman. One young artist named Devære, a Frenchman, had followed him to Rome, and he had a definite agreement with Wedgwood which included a salary and additional payment for any models that he should supply, with another clause in it which allowed him to seek and execute any work for others, and so enable him to establish a business for himself there. He sent many models to Etruria, to some of which Wedgwood raised objection because of the nakedness of the figures, for beautiful as he admitted they were, he pointed out that it was absolutely necessary to clothe them if they were to be of use to him for introduction into furniture in England. Wedgwood pointed out that this increased the labour upon them and required the hand of an experienced master, and finally that when done the piece would cease to be a copy from the antique.

The models mentioned in connection with Devære's name are : " The Discovery of Achilles," " The History of Orestes," " The Judgment of Paris."

It is quite certain that Devære worked directly under Flaxman's eye, and that some of the work that was sent to Etruria had finishing touches put to it by Flaxman, who in a letter to Byerley mentions specially the basrelief of the Borghese Vase in which Devære has succeeded very well, but after he has done " I shall have something to do to it."

When Webber was in Rome at the same time as Flaxman was there, he made excursions to search for subjects that could be modelled to suit Wedgwood, and for this purpose he engaged the services of a group of artists, whose names were Angelo Dalmazzoni, Pacetti, Angelini, Manzolini, Fratoddi, Mangiarotti, and Cades, who, while he remained in Rome, received instructions and payment from him, but after he left an English resident named Jenkins transacted all such business, which was referred to either Greek Street [1] or Etruria. These basrelief models were very numerous (some of the wax originals are in Etruria Museum to-day, showing in an interesting way the damage received in packing, which was one of Wedgwood's complaints), but although it is believed that the names of the modellers were attached to them when they first came, no record now exists and it is not possible to say with certainty whose work they are. This has been attempted, but no more can be said. They were the work of the above-named artists, and probably were passed and approved by Flaxman before they were sent to England, which would account for the question being brought before him as the responsible head in Wedgwood's letter of February 1790.

Lady Templetown [2] gave Wedgwood permission to use one of her drawings of a group to make a basrelief subject of it for a cameo, and when this was finished it was submitted to her by his nephew Byerley, which received her approval, and called forth the thanks of Wedgwood in a letter to her, the draft of which is preserved. " Mr W. presents his most respectfull

[1] The London showroom of Wedgwood & Bentley.
[2] This name has generally been spelt " Templeton," but her own letter to Wedgwood in August 1790 from Summerhill, her residence, gives the name as " Templetown."

" comp[ts] to Lady Templetown & is very happy to learn
" by his nephew M[r] Byerley that his attempt to copy
" in bas relief the charming groups of little figures her
" ladyship was so obliging as to lend him has met with
" that approbation which he durst not flatter himself
" with, & is sensible he owes much to Lady Templetowns
" politeness on this occasion. M[r] Wedgwood is afraid
" to trespass farther upon the goodness he has already
" experienc'[d], & is sensible that nothing but experience
" could justify his expressing a wish to be indulged in
" copying a few more such groups, but however earnest
" his wishes may be, he begs to be understood to
" express them with the most perfect submissions to
" L. T[s] pleasure." [1]   After this, several other subjects
were modelled from her Ladyship's designs.

A great number were the smaller frieze subjects of
domestic scenes, and Amorini, but as her designs are
similar to others supplied, more especially those by
Miss Crew, it is impossible to separate them.

Lady Diana Beauclerk is represented in some of the
Infant Bacchanalian groups and figures, which were
used chiefly in oval placques, and upon some flowerpots
and pedestals for vases of later period.

The portrait medallions modelled by the " Gossets "
were acquired by Wedgwood to reproduce in his Jasper
medallion series of " Illustrious Moderns " and were not
modelled directly for him. The same must be said of
the portraits taken from the medals of Dassier and
Pingo, both of whom were connected with the Mint.

George Stubbs, R.A., was the artist who painted

[1] Draft of a letter, Wedgwood to Lady Templetown, June 27,
1783.

portraits of both Josiah Wedgwood and Mrs. Wedgwood and the family group, in the grounds of Etruria Hall, beside other portraits of the gentry of the neighbourhood. He was resident during these periods at Etruria and in this way became interested in the work of the modelling studio at the works.

His desire to model some subjects for Wedgwood is referred to in a letter : " He sleeps with us & wishes to " employ some of his evenings in modelling a com " panion to his frighten'd horse, & has fixed upon one " of his Phætons for that purpose." [1] The subject of this placque is the one known as " The Fall of Phæton." There are at Etruria the original wax models (damaged) and the block moulds of sixteen cameo subjects of single horses that can also be assigned to this artist.

The work of many of the famous artists and sculptors of Wedgwood's day appears in some form upon his ware, but it is not correct to say that they all worked or even supplied designs directly to him. Any subject available that commended itself as suitable for reproduction in pottery was readily accepted and carried out by the modellers at Etruria. In this way the Infant Academy of Sir Joshua Reynolds was produced, and subjects after Stothard and others.

Invoices for models supplied have misled in many cases. If those from Mrs. Landre and Grant & Hoskins, and even John Flaxman, are considered carefully, it will be found that they are not the bills for work done by an artist or sculptor, but only an account rendered for goods supplied in the form of casts taken from the antique, and other sources.

[1] Wedgwood to Bentley, October 28, 1780.

The first account of Flaxman to Wedgwood in 1775, which has been quoted so often, containing the models of the Wine and Water Ewers will, in the opinion of the author, have to be placed among this class, and will upset the long-cherished theory that these models were Flaxman's original work. The probability is that they were just casts from the antique supplied by Flaxman senior and adapted by Wedgwood to his purpose.

This view is strengthened by the fact that the receipting of the account is " for my father " and this list of models scarcely looks like the original work of a young man of twenty years.

In the same way the accounts of Mrs. Landre and Messrs. Grant and Hoskins must be viewed ; they were only plaster-cast dealers and not modellers employed by Wedgwood, as has been so repeatedly said.

IX

COLOURED BODIES
OTHER WARES
CHINA
MARKS

CHAPTER IX

COLOURED BODIES AND OTHER WARES

**The various coloured " bodies " made at Etruria—Pearl
" body "—The Red " body "—Cane-coloured " body "—
The Drab " body "—The Lavender " body "—The mark
upon modern pieces—The great variety of wares—
Useful ware made for Royalty—Chemical ware and
mortars—Tiles—Slabs for artists to paint upon—The
uses that Jasper was put to for mounting—Tobacco
pipes—The set of chessmen—" Moonlight " lustre—The
marks found upon Wedgwood Ware—Workmen's tools.**

COLOURED ware has been made at Etruria, that is to
say, self-coloured bodies. Apart from the jasper
ware, basaltes, and cream colour, there were other
coloured clays that were somewhat extensively used.

The jasper coloured clays used for making the ware
were white, black, pale blue and a slate grey blue ;
the other colours being introduced as dips or washes in
the form of slip, which only gave a surface veneer of
coloured clay upon the solid white body. These were
always used in conjunction with decoration in white
relief of figures, or leafage, etc. When a plain black
undecorated piece was desired, it was always made
in the basaltes body.

The earthenware body was the Queensware or cream
colour, and any embossed ornament upon it was
generally in the mould and pressed with it in making,
except in some special fancy pieces such as vases or

flowerpots, inkstands, etc., that received the relief
decoration in the same manner as the jasper ware,
the ornaments being made in a separate mould and
applied upon the piece in clay and finished by hand.
A white body, made to approach the effect of china in
colour was made later but used almost entirely for table
ware, it was called " Pearl " body, and was introduced
chiefly to give the cobalt used in painting or printing
a brighter colour than could be obtained on the cream
coloured body. This was introduced about 1779.
Printing fully engraved patterns was not done at
Wedgwood's Works until 1805. However, the copper
engraved plate and transfer print was in use before
that, but only to supply the outline of crests or coats of
arms, or subjects which were afterwards fully painted so
as in most cases to cover up any mechanically produced
outline, the object being to have uniformity of size of
the pattern and avoid bad drawing, as well as to save
the time which would otherwise have been necessary
in laboriously outlining in pencil the same design
upon a number of pieces, as in a dinner service.

A red body had been made by almost every potter,
and was looked upon as a common ware, although
Elers had elevated it into a very highly finished article
in his beautiful little teapots and jugs. Wedgwood
made a very good red body, and used it for some quite
elaborate pieces, making a series of Etruscan shapes,
some plain and others decorated with relief figures in
black. It was, however, mainly used to make ordinary
useful ware, such as teapots, jugs, etc., and as such it
was always regarded by Wedgwood. In one of his
letters to Bentley he writes : " You recommend red

1.   2.

1. CAN AND SAUCER, EARTHENWARE, " MOONLIGHT " LUSTRE.
(Wedgwood Institute, Burslem.)

2. CUP AND SAUCER, CHINA (*circa* 1812).
(British Museum.)

3.

4.

3. BROTH BOWL AND STAND, DRAB EARTHENWARE.

4. JUG, DRAB EARTHENWARE, WITH GOLD BAND ROUND RIM.
(Etruria Museum.)

[*To face page* 228.

BOWL, CANE BODY, "BAMBOO" PATTERN, WITH ENAMEL
PAINTED DECORATION.

(Victoria and Albert Museum.)

INKSTAND, RED BODY, WITH WHITE RELIEF.

(Etruria Museum.)

[*To face page* 229.

" clay for Cabinet heads, My objection to it is the
" extreme vulgarity of red wares. If it had never
" been made in T. pots and the commonest wares my
" objection would not have existed, But as it will be
" necessary they should be sold cheap & we should
" give some obvious reason for that cheapness, this
" alone may render it proper to make them in red
" clay." [1] The name that was given to this red body
was " Rosso Antico," but its high-sounding appellation
never obliterated its identity in Wedgwood's eyes, and
he was never very enthusiastic about it. " I wish you
" would fix upon one of the Bronze like colors for
" Heads," he writes, " as we shall never be able to
" make the Rosso Antico otherwise than to put you
" in mind of a Red-Pot Teapot." [2] Bentley must
have been very keen upon having it, for the matter is
not allowed to rest, and a further reply drives home
the same prejudice once more : " I will try to imitate
" the Antico Rosso from your description, but when I
" have done my best I am afraid where one spectator
" thinks of Antico Rosso an hundred will be put in
" mind of a Red Teapot." [3]
The red body, however, was used, and variations in
colour to a deep chocolate were produced.

A fine inkstand is illustrated showing a relief design
in white upon red, period 1820, the second Josiah ;
there are very few of these pieces known, and it is not
likely that many were made. (See illus. facing p. 229.)

A greater range of black relief upon red are known,

[1] Wedgwood to Bentley, January 4, 1776.
[2] Ibid., March 3, 1776.
[3] Ibid., March 10, 1776.

but this must be placed to a later date and includes all the Egyptian hieroglyphic designs which belong to the same period.

Cane coloured body is one of the original clays and was a refined material prepared from the local marl of the district. It was a material that gave some amount of trouble, which was not easily overcome. Figures as well as ware were made in it. In 1779 we have a reference, " We have made Voltaire & R. . . . " in cane colour ready to firing. They will have the " appearance of models, & to strengthen that idea in " the very offset I would not shew more than one " pair in the rooms at a time. Our present cane " colour body is very imperfect. It has a coarse " speckled appearance if examin'd with attention. Is " very porous, & apt to stain. I have not yet been " able to give it a porcelain texture, & preserve its " color : but if I live I hope to compass it." [1] The firing caused it to stain, and so a good piece of work in other ways was spoilt by discoloration. " We cover'd " them close in burning, knowing how apt this body is " to turn brown, but in vain." [2]

However, this difficulty was mastered and a very extensive range of useful ware was made in cane, which is a beautiful specimen of thin potting, having delicate finishing on the " fluting " or engine turning lathe. This ware was often further decorated with enamel painting. (See illus. facing p. 229.)

The " Drab " body was introduced about 1820, and is only found in useful ware ; very occasionally pieces,

[1] Wedgwood to Bentley, September 26, 1779.
[2] *Ibid.*, October 16, 1779.

or even tea sets, or dessert sets, are found which have a printed pattern carefully filled in with colours in the Oriental manner.

This ware is always beautifully " potted," but apart from an odd cream jug or such-like small piece is not likely to interest the collector.

The " Lavender " body was not introduced until about the middle of the nineteenth century, and the " Flemish " body later still. Both are represented almost entirely by table ware and generally quite plain, very few pieces have been decorated, even with an edge line.

A grey body (named " Oriental ") and grey-green body (named " Chinese "), used for table ware only, are quite a modern product, having been made only during the last twenty years, but some collectors, finding the name upon it and the technique and finish, coupled with the old shape and design, have concluded it was old. It is thought advisable to put the matter right in this volume. On such pieces a date mark will always be found, in the form of a private mark, which is a combination of three block letters, sometimes a figure and two letters. This mark is impressed on the clay, and is only for reference at the works, indicating the cycle or private mark, the workman's mark and the year mark respectively. This plan of marking all useful ware was started in 1860. There are also single impressed letters upon the clay which refer to the month of the year in which the piece was made, or the particular " body " of which it was made. When " Pearl " body was first introduced the name PEARL was impressed in full in the clay.

When a collector begins to take an interest in Wedgwood, surprise is expressed at the great variety of wares and styles there are that came out of the different factories under his control. Beside the ordinary table wares, vases in both jasper, basaltes, and cream colour, placques, medallions, cameos, and intaglios, we find quite a number of side interests, to each of which he gave his attention and skill with a thoroughness that characterised all his work. Kitchen and dairy ware received much careful thought, which resulted in a series of utensils absolutely fitted to their uses, and whose practical qualities are not superseded to-day. In some old county families at the home farm the settling pans for cream that were made by Josiah are still in use to-day. Our Queen has some pieces of such utilitarian ware which were made originally for Queen Charlotte, the wife of George III. These have been in use probably in a dairy. These pieces are decorated with a painted ivy wreath border.

Chemical ware has always been made at Etruria, the mortars and pestles especially being highly praised by those who have to use them. This branch was one into which Wedgwood put his best. As with everything, so with this, he was the pioneer and had to discover his materials, then prove them; this acid proof, porcelain body proved as tiresome as many of the others, but he never let a half-good article pass—it must be the best. After a long description of his difficulties in this respect in one of his letters to Bentley, he writes : " This occasions an unavoidable interruption " in your supply of mortars, but perfection being our

" aim in all things, we must not stop too far short of
" it even in mortars." [1]

Tiles in cream colour glazed ware were an introduction
in the early days while the works were still at Burslem,
and are first referred to in 1767. " Cream colour Tyle
" are much wanted, & the consumption will be great
" for Dairys, Baths, Summer Houses, Temples, &c.,
" &c. This Article will come under the Ornamental
" Class, & you may be looking out for a sober Tyle
" maker amongst your Potthouses to bring along
" with you." [2]

" Lady Gower will build a dairy on purpose to
" furnish it with Cream Couler if I will engage to make
" Tiles for the Walls." [3]

The matter was not dropped, but developed slowly.
We find that experiments were made for both floor
and wall tiles and in jasper as well as cream colour.
" Patterns of Bricks for a Jasper floor 9 squares long
" by 6 broad, with a border of Porphyry and Black
" ones sufficient for one side and one end. N°. 1. 2
" & 3 are first attempts for makeing Tiles for Baths
" &c. They will be made pretty expeditiously, &
" borders of different colours may be made to form
" them into compartments &c." [4]

During this year the fashion for using tiles in bath-
rooms and dairies seems to have developed, and
Wedgwood took it up in conjunction with Mr. Green,
of Sadler & Green, to supply printed cream colour
tiles in designs forming panels.

[1] Wedgwood to Bentley, May 30, 1779.
[2] Ibid., August 5, 1767.
[3] Ibid., September 17, 1769.
[4] Ibid., June 26, 1776.

It is interesting to note in how many ways the genius of Wedgwood was utilized; he acquired a reputation for an ability to tackle any ceramic problem, and was generally willing to do so, if any hopes of success suggested itself.

One excursion into a strange province was the making of earthenware slabs for artists to paint upon. Mr. George Stubbs, R.A., was desirous of having some, and his demands at first were evidently rather in excess of the ability to supply. " My comp^{ts} to Mr. " Stubbs. He shall be gratified but large Tablets are " not the work of a day. We have been labouring at " an apparatus for that purpose from the day I came " down, & can report some progress." [1]

One or two were made 22 inches by 17 inches, and others were tried larger, but the report is that only one was perfect ; still nothing daunted, larger ones were tried.

Here again continual trial and experiment won at last, but not until two years had elapsed. We have an intermediate note which tells of disappointment, as well as endeavour to excel : " When you see M^r " Stubs pray tell him how hard I have been labouring " to furnish him with the means of adding immortality " to his very excellent pencil. I mean only to arrogate " to myself the honor of being his canvas maker. " But alass this honor is at present denied to my en- " deavours, though you may assure him that I will " succeed if I live a while longer." [2]

Eight months after the record is : " We shall be able

---

[1] Wedgwood to Bentley, November 4, 1777.
[2] *Ibid.*, October 17, 1778.

" now to make them with certainty & success of the
" size of the 3 in this inv? & I hope soon to say as far
" as 30 inches,—perhaps ultimately up to 36 inches by
" 24.   If M! Stubbs succeeds he will be followed by
" others, & if the oil painters too should use them
" they may become a considerable object." [1]

A palette of nineteen colours in enamel was prepared
for painting on these tablets, and portraits of Mr.
and Mrs. Wedgwood were executed in them.   There is
no doubt that other pictures were painted ; some few
have already been seen (one, a portrait on an oval
slab 18 inches by 12, is in Etruria Museum), so that it
is not unlikely that more may yet be discovered.

In searching for Wedgwood Ware, one is continually
surprised by the discovery of some hitherto unknown
use that it was made to serve ; tributaries, as it were,
to the main stream were explored and navigated as
far as possible.   In this way we come across the most
dainty pieces of jasper ware used alone, or mounted in
metal for the old-fashioned bell-pulls, cylindrical drums
with the minutest detail of relief work, forming the
casing for single and double opera-glasses.   Beads
and buttons of all shapes and sizes were also made,
as well as cameo pieces pierced all round the edge with
small holes to allow of stitching them on to material
as a feature in an embroidery design, or for introducing into a lace pattern.

Door knobs, and handles for cabinet doors, finger
and escutcheon plates, form quite an interesting,
though perhaps quite a small, group to-day, as so many
of these very exquisitely finished pieces have been

[1] Wedgwood to Bentley, May 20, 1779.

divorced from their original surroundings, and appear somewhat meaningless. Many of these curious shapes will be accounted for by their original positions in sword hilts, long earrings, buckles for shoes, and clasps for belts or cloaks.

Tobacco pipes in cream colour, red, and jasper, in fair numbers, were produced during the Wedgwood & Bentley period and appear in the sale catalogue in 1781. Hookahs and chibouques were made after 1800, and to this period belong also the " Staithes " patent pipe heads.

The set of chessmen modelled by Flaxman is an instance of the use which was made of the jasper " body." The original drawing for this set is at Etruria, as well as seven of the wax models ; unfortunately only one is at all perfect, a queen—generally supposed to be Mrs. Siddons as Lady Macbeth—all the others being headless.

The drawing was made and sent to Etruria in 1785, and the models made soon after.

Many complete sets were issued, the figures being made in blue jasper and white jasper upon different coloured plinths. As many as 130 sets were made between 1785 and 1795.

Lustre ware was not made until the beginning of the nineteenth century, when some very beautiful effects were produced, including the one which has since been called " Moonlight." (See illus. facing p. 228.) The metallic decoration of the eighteenth century, which has been termed silver and gold lustre, is not correctly named, for it is only metal applied as a pigment with a brush.

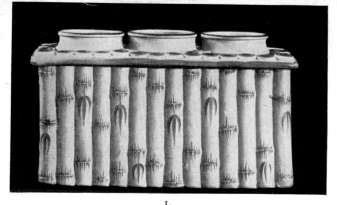

I.

2.

3.

4.

6.

7.

I. POT FOR GROWING BULBS, CANE BODY, "BAMBOO" PATTERN,
ENAMEL PAINTED DECORATION.

2 & 3. POTTER'S STAMPS FOR MARKING WARE IN CLAY STATE.

4 & 5. OTHER VIEWS OF 2 & 3, ONE MARKED "LOWNDS" AND
DATED "1789," THE OTHER "JAMES PATTISON" AND
DATED "1783."

6. A RIB OR PROFILE FOR MAKING A BOWL OR CUP, MARKED
"JNO. GREAVES, 1795."

7 A JASPER TABLET USED BY WEDGWOOD WHEN EXHIBITING
HIS VASES.

(Etruria Museum.)

[To face page 236.

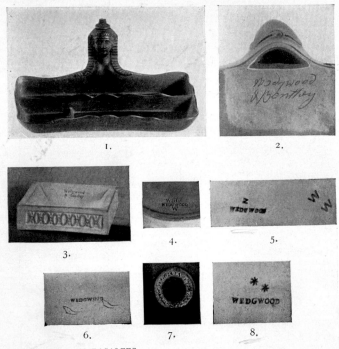

1. PEN TRAY IN BASALTES.
2. UNIQUE SCRIPT MARK "WEDGWOOD & BENTLEY," ON NO. 1.
3 & 7. "WEDGWOOD & BENTLEY" MARKS.
4. "WEDGWOOD" MARK, SHOWING THE DATE MARK.
5, 6 & 8. EARLY MARKS ON EARTHENWARE, PRIOR TO DATE MARKING.

(Etruria Museum.)

[To face page 237.

China was never made during the first Josiah's lifetime, although he had made various experiments and trials for producing it. It was introduced at Etruria in 1812 and continued to be made, mainly in teaware, until 1815, when it was discontinued owing to the rush of orders that came to the works for earthenware after the Battle of Waterloo. Some of this china teaware was richly decorated with coloured patterns and gold. The illustration given is plain white with an embossed vine-leaf pattern and a gold band round the rim. (See illus. facing p. 228.)

The marks found upon Wedgwood Ware are very numerous, but the essential one to collectors is very uniform. The first mark of importance is Wedgwood & Bentley and occurs on ware manufactured during that partnership, which existed between 1769 and 1780, and was used in full impressed with type arranged as :—

No. 3 in varying sizes.

The other form was upon a lozenge of clay applied on to the foot or plinth of a piece, either in the centre to admit of a screw being put through for fixing the several pieces of the vase together, or as shown in illustrations.

The only variation used was an abbreviated form " W. & B." in different sizes for stamping upon small pieces such as cameos and intaglios.

The script mark, " Wedgwood & Bentley " (see illus. facing p. 237) is the only one known, and occurs on the pen tray illustrated here, which is in the museum at Etruria. The spigot on the head of the sphinx originally had a nozzle to hold a taper for sealing letters.

The plain word " Wedgwood " has been used since 1771, during the partnership period for useful ware, and afterwards continuously until the present day.

All other marks, single letters and stamps of various devices refer to the manufacture, and are makers' (potters') marks, or denote the " body," colour, etc., of the piece. When three letters are found in combination it indicates that the piece has been made since 1860, the first letter being the private mark or cycle, the second the potter's mark, and the third the year mark.

The three marks 5–6–8 (see illus. facing p. 237) all

belong to the early part of the nineteenth century, before the yearly mark was introduced, and show the name and the stamp used by the potter who made the piece.

The tools of workmen have an interest which may be touched upon here, especially as those illustrated have a date as well as a name upon them. (See illus. facing p. 236.)

These tools are handed down from father to son, and workman to workman, many having been in use for considerably over a hundred years.

X

CHRONOLOGICAL
DETAILS

CHAPTER X

CHRONOLOGICAL DETAILS

The different wares produced by Wedgwood in the order of their appearance from 1759 to 1850—Incidents of the appreciation of Wedgwood's work recorded a hundred years after his death.

ANY attempt to give a chronological list of Wedgwood's work is difficult, because so much of it overlapped and, as will be seen from the foregoing chapters, the endeavours to perfect a particular section of his efforts occupied the space of several years, during which time periods of success were experienced that again and again had to give way to similar periods when failure seemed to be the only prospect in view.

However, some slight record may be found helpful, and this will be in a form dated by the years during which he carried on his work as a manufacturer.

1759   The works at Ivy House were started and
to   small articles chiefly were made, such as knife-
1764. hafts, spoons, snuffboxes, and articles for the hardware manufacturers of Birmingham and Sheffield.

     " Pineapple " and " Cauliflower " ware was made, probably in large quantities.

     The first pieces of engine-turned ware were produced at this period.   (See illus. facing p. 68.)

Improvements in cream coloured ware and the first complete services made.

Vases and ornamental pieces of large size in cream colour. (See illus. facing p. 69.)

Printed patterns were used upon the cream coloured ware services ; the printing was done by Sadler & Green at Liverpool. (See illus. facing p. 85.)

" Marbled," " agate," and " onyx " vases. (See illus. facing p. 75.)

1764 to 1769.   At the Brick House works the same class of ware was made ; the increase in the useful ware (cream colour) grew so rapidly that all the ornamental department was removed to the new works at Etruria as soon as they were ready. Although the ornamental ware department of the works was removed, the useful ware part remained and was carried on in this factory until 1773. The " Cauliflower " and " Pineapple " wares being included in the useful ware department, remained behind and were not made at all at Etruria. This may also be said of the smaller wares referred to above.

1769.   Upon entering the new works at Etruria, attention was centred on the production of the finer ornamental wares, vases especially, and Bentley in this year became Wedgwood's partner.

From this time date the first of the medallions, placques, and cameos in cream colour, bisque, red and black, the relief figure and background being of the same colour.

Black basaltes vases with Etruscan painting upon them are first introduced, and command a great sale.

The quest for material for designs to furnish the increase in the number of vases is carried on enthusiastically.

1769　The cabinets of nobility and gentry are opened to supply the want. The trouble with Voyez commences.

The first day's "throwing" at Etruria, June 13th. Wedgwood himself "threw" the vases while Bentley, his partner, turned the wheel.

Mr. and Mrs. Wilcox (painters) first hired, who afterwards went to Chelsea and worked upon the great Russian Service for the Empress Catherine II.

Tiles for dairies, etc., in cream colour first asked for and made.

Terra-cotta figures begun.

Hackwood started (an ingenious boy).

Vases made in imitation of variegated pebble introduced.

Sir Wm. Hamilton's book on Etruscan vases acquired, and shapes copied from it.

Bronze encaustic first made.

First dealings with Tassie.

Candlestick vases first made ; these were the reversible ones, similar to the one shown on illustration facing p. 138.

1770.   Lions and sphinxes in the making, also tritons and elephants, as well as a few figures of boys.

The Duke of Marlborough's gems consulted.

Development of the " Pebble " vase range.

Pyramid flowerpots and large milk pans.

Additions to the basrelief subjects.

1771.   Greek and Roman heads series.

Sphinx tripods.

Busts from the antique.

Printed and yellow ground teaware.

Knife handles and red teapots still being made at the Burslem Works.

1772.   New lamps, other than the tripod and sphinx, of plainer shape made.

Many additions to the gems made.

" Bow pots " (bough pots) introduced instead of making cheap vases.

Tablets started.

Gem cameos made for mounting in snuff-boxes, etc.

1773.   Cabinets made with sets of historical heads.

Seals made—sales good—catalogue made.

Order for Russian Service received.

Sale of tablets commences.

First trials for a leadless glaze.

1774.   Cream colour ordered more than ever.

Basaltes " will last for ever."

The busts arrive at Etruria.
The making of portrait medallions increases.
The Jasper " body " matures.
Blue and black onyx intaglios made.

1775. Jasper " body " perfected in white, blue, and sea-green.
Tablets for chimney pieces.
First mention of Flaxman. Work executed by him.
Six modellers working at basreliefs.

1776. Large tablets successful.
Tablet subjects in hand.
The French medallion portraits.
Basrelief vases made but not offered for sale (these were basaltes vases with relief figures).
Red, black, and bronze tablets made.

1777. The " washed " coloured ground for heads instead of the solid coloured ground introduced and pronounced better and finer.
Flaxman's " Muses " modelled.
Tablets for Longton Hall made.

1778. Green hooped flowerpots (Devonshire flower-pots).
Tablets and heads very successful.
Studying conchology.
Jasper figures for architects.

1779.   " Illustrious Moderns " series increases.
The " Pearl " body first made.
The " Virgil " bust.

1780   From 1780 to 1790 was the best period for
to   all classes of ware that was made at Etruria.
1790.   A steady increase in the variety of subjects and
number of shapes produced, as well as the
closest attention to technique and finish.

1786.   It is not easy to mark especially any pieces,
with the exception of the arrival of the
" Portland Vase," being sent in this year
for the purpose of copying.

In the same year the " Homeric Vase,"
mentioned in Wedgwood's letter to Sir Wm.
Hamilton, was presented by Wedgwood to
the British Museum.

1787.   The introduction of ornamental cameos in
many colours, and the making of buttons,
all in most minute and exquisite detail.

1790.   The first " Portland Vase " came out to the
satisfaction of Wedgwood.

Basaltes ware with silver borders.

1805.   Lustres on earthenware date from this year.
Printing full patterns in blue for dinner and
tea services.

Egyptian hieroglyphic relief patterns modelled
about this time.

1810.   A smear glaze introduced on earthenware,
often mistaken for salt glaze.

1812. China first made at Etruria.

1816. Making of china ceased, to be renewed only in 1878.

1832. Hackwood retired from the works.

1836. Hackwood died.

1838. A cheap edition of the "Portland Vase" made in all sizes, cast in one piece, with the background painted in with enamel colour after bisque firing.

1843. Josiah II's death. This ended the second period, during which time a continual flow of all the good patterns was maintained and many new jasper vases were introduced.

From 1800 to 1816 jasper products and sales increased greatly, to slacken off later.

1845. The "Lavender" earthenware "body" introduced.

1850. A revival of Jasper commenced.

Cream colour continued without any break and also Basaltes in both useful and ornamental pieces.

During Wedgwood's lifetime he enjoyed the friendship of a great many of the cultured influential men of the period, and Royalty and nobility sought him

out to express their appreciation of his work and add
their patronage to the long list. This expression came
from all parts of the world, for his name was revered
outside his native country, and it exists to-day.

At the time when the centenary of Wedgwood's
death was celebrated by an exhibition of his works
at Burslem, the firm of Josiah Wedgwood & Sons
received a wreath direct from a potter in Silesia,
with the request that it should be placed upon the
great potter's grave, as a remembrance from a living
potter to the memory of one who was universally
esteemed as the greatest master of his craft.

An incident quite worth recording occurred just
lately in the Museum at Etruria. A Chinese gentleman of position was paying a visit to the Potteries
and included Etruria in his programme. After being
shown round the old works, he entered the Museum,
and the portrait medallion, life size, of Josiah Wedgwood was pointed out to him. He solemnly and
reverently stopped, and in Oriental manner made
obeisance to it, bowing low six times in succession
before he proceeded on his tour of inspection.

INDEX

INDEX

Printed in Great Britain by
UNWIN BROTHERS, LIMITED, LONDON AND WOKING